Regarding the real

Manchester University Press

Regarding the real

Cinema, documentary, and the visual arts

Des O'Rawe

Manchester University Press

The right of Des O'Rawe to be identified as the author of this work has been asserted by him in accordance with the Copyright, Designs and Patents Act 1988.

Published by Manchester University Press
Altrincham Street, Manchester M1 7JA

www.manchesteruniversitypress.co.uk

British Library Cataloguing-in-Publication Data
A catalogue record for this book is available from the British Library

Library of Congress Cataloging-in-Publication Data applied for

ISBN 978 0 7190 9966 3 hardback

First published 2016

The publisher has no responsibility for the persistence or accuracy of URLs for any external or third-party internet websites referred to in this book, and does not guarantee that any content on such websites is, or will remain, accurate or appropriate.

Typeset by
Servis Filmsetting Ltd, Stockport, Cheshire
Printed in Great Britain
by TJ International Ltd, Padstow

To Deirdre, and the boys

,

Contents

Illustrations

Images in this book are screen grabs which are reproduced
here under the fair dealing guidelines relating to criticism
and review as suggested by the Intellectual Property Office
(published 12 June 2014).

Acknowledgements

This book originated while I was teaching a module on cinema and the visual arts. I was encouraged to teach that module, and persuaded to write this book, by Sam Rohdie.

My thinking on matters herein and elsewhere has been sharpened by regular caffeine-fuelled conversations with Francis Hagan – in a café with a bookshop that was once a bookshop with a café. I am also grateful to Nigel Harkness, Eamonn Hughes, Peter Kane, Geoffrey Nowell-Smith, Mark Phelan, Jim Smyth, and Rod Stoneman. A word of thanks is also owed to Raymond Armstrong, Sîan Barber, Stefano Baschiera, Marina Burke, Elena Carduro, Paula Blair, Al Fisher, Glenn Gallagher, Fiona Handyside, Declan Keeney, Cahal McLaughlin, Richard O'Sullivan, and Gary D. Rhodes.

Earlier versions of parts of this book have appeared in print as follows: *Quarterly Review of Film and Video*, 29 (1); *Studies in Documentary Film*, 5 (1); and *Film Quarterly*, 66 (1). A Leverhulme Research Fellowship enabled me to complete the manuscript in 2013–14, and the School of Creative Arts at Queen's allowed me to take advantage of that opportunity.

Introduction

Jean-Luc Godard has always treated categorical definitions of the documentary with scepticism: 'All great fiction films tend towards documentary, just as all great documentaries tend toward fiction.'[1] The filmmakers discussed in this book are unlikely to refute such a statement. Encompassing an enquiry into the fictive and phenomenological nature of the documentary image, their films are never simply illustrative of a script or complicit in the pretence of coherence: theirs is an associative and fragmentary film language, a language that subverts the conventions of documentary realism, and contradicts commonplace assumptions about reality and its representation.

Nowadays, an extensive body of critical literature on the relations between cinema and the visual arts tends to concentrate on three areas of enquiry: comparative conceptual or historical issues; questions of representation and *mise en scène* in narrative–commercial cinema; and convergences between the avant-garde and wider film culture. Sometimes, these areas will overlap, especially in debates around the role of new media technologies and how they blur the boundaries between film, video, photography, and installation art. However, even when studying formally inventive documentaries that engage explicitly with the other visual arts, the prevailing critical methodology, especially within the Anglo-American tradition, prefers the cinema of cultural studies to a cultural studies of the cinema, so to speak.[2] While *Regarding the Real: Cinema, Documentary, and the Visual Arts* also considers how some documentaries depict modern artists, artworks, and histories of art, it is more interested in addressing a different question: how are documentary filmmaking styles shaped by ideas, materials, and expressive techniques derived from the modern visual arts?

Taking its bearings from forms of writing that encourage a creative symbiosis between criticism and art, the book's style is essayistic, shaped as much by intuition as by erudition. Covering a period that extends from the 1930s to 1980s, it frames a particular coincidence of preoccupations, concepts, affinities, and serendipities. This time-frame is loose but not arbitrary: ranging from the institutionalisation of synchronous sound to the advent of video production, it delineates an epoch of sorts, or *episteme*. After all, this period also extends from the rise of fascism to the final throes of the Cold War. As such, it encompasses an intellectual and social landscape associated with so-called 'late modernism', and the films discussed often involve major cities of modernism at historically eventful junctures (London, New York, Amsterdam, Paris, Tokyo, or Barcelona), rendering them as mosaics of shapes, spaces, and incidental gestures rather than monumental and pristine metropolises of high modernity. These films also tend to be products of an artisanal rather than a commercial imperative, frequently incorporating found footage, and fragments from alternative image systems, into their documentary *mise en scène*. In many cases, they may even be more familiar to students of animation, assemblage and collage, photography, or post-war film modernism, than to students of the documentary.

As figures who can relate to cinema through other arts, the filmmakers discussed in *Regarding the Real* convey an ambitious, experimental sense of what the documentary can achieve artistically, and what it can offer its audiences as a visual art form in its own right. This is filmmaking as a question of framing, cutting, and assembling, as an exercise in the imaginative arrangement of images and sounds, and not filmmaking as an afterthought, or lightweight vehicle for the transportation of stories.

The opening chapter looks at Len Lye's career with the General Post Office (GPO) Film Unit during the 1930s. It situates his work at this time within a broader contemporary visual culture, and attempts to clarify the nature and extent of his contribution to the British documentary tradition. In particular, it examines how his filmmaking incorporated promotional advertising and commercial art techniques while remaining amenable to avant-garde abstraction and kinaesthetic experimentation. Lye's GPO films – like those of Norman McLaren, Lotte Reiniger, and Humphrey Jennings – complicate assumptions about the Documentary Movement of the inter-war era, and its relations to film and modernism in Britain. John Grierson's tendency to overemphasise the instrumentalist and realist achievements of the documentary at this time was both politically pragmatic and culturally myopic: '[Grierson] adapted film's radical potential to far less radical ends'.[3] There was an anarchic and restless quality to Lye's career, and while he was by no means the only modernist associated with the GPO Film Unit, the extent of his ability to innovate – in spite of meagre production budgets – with colour processes, musical compositions, stencils, and found footage is remarkable. In a comment to Roger Horrocks, Alberto Cavalcanti – who produced some of Lye's films, and had himself been active in European avant-garde film culture in the 1920s – encapsulated how Lye was both an asset and an affront to Grierson's project: 'Len Lye could be described in the history of British cinema by one word – experiment.'[4]

Like Lye, Joseph Cornell was also a pioneer of found footage filmmaking, although his New York films of the 1950s were not produced within an established production unit, or commissioned by commercial companies. Cornell's documentaries are an extension of his collage and assemblage art – as well as his better known experiments from the 1930s (for example, *Rose Hobart* (1936, 19 min.)) – and their uncanny documentary forms flicker between realism and symbolism, materiality and mystery. Just as Lye's work is related to London's broader artistic and literary environment during the inter-war period, so too Cornell's techniques are not unrelated to the work of the artists, writers, and composers associated with the New York School. In discussing Cornell's films in this context, the second chapter in this book emphasises several converging critical contexts: first, the visual – especially, photographic –

culture developing in New York in the 1950s, a culture that included Cornell, even if he did not, officially, belong to any of its coteries; second, the people he worked with on these films, especially his collaborations with Rudy Burckhardt and Stan Brakhage, and their respective connections to the New York School and the city's burgeoning avant-garde scene; third, how – in formal terms – Cornell's films from the 1950s relate to his other artwork, especially, the boxes, assemblages, the collage–montage films of the 1930s, and his artistic vision, more generally; and, finally, the relevance of these films to a broader discussion on documentary practice and its relation to the modern visual arts.

While these opening chapters focus on the relations between documentary forms and various – especially, surrealist-orientated – techniques and contexts, the next two chapters elaborate on the role of photography, exploring how it shaped the documentary filmmaking of Johan van der Keuken and William Klein. The montage structure of the chapter on Van der Keuken is itself based on a photo album, in which each of the films discussed is linked to the preceding film. Given that his film and photographic work is characterised by an array of influences – and that his visual style and sensibility was marked by a reticent attitude towards notions of coher-ence and finality – framing, in the broadest sense – such a structure seems appropriate in this case. This cross-section of Van der Keuken's film *œuvre* is treated chiefly in terms of how it develops, and subverts, conventional documentary frames of reference, and attempts to transcend the problem of rendering a reality that is always elusive, and a representation that is always inadequate. Furthermore, just as London and New York feature as more than a backdrop to the chapters on Lye and Cornell, so too this chapter emphasises the impor-tance of Amsterdam's artistic communities and contemporary history to Van der Keuken's imagination. Despite his many travels around the world, there is always a sense in his films that Amsterdam – like Marco Polo's Venice in Italo Calvino's *Invisible Cities/Le città invisibili* (1972) – is everywhere, and everywhere, sooner or later, becomes Amsterdam.

As in the case of Van der Keuken, it is interesting to consider William Klein's filmmaking in relation to his photography, and how he too uses different documentary forms to investigate the relations between time and movement, image and montage. In a career now spanning over sixty years (at the time of writing), Klein's work also testifies to a remarkable range of influences: Dada and surrealism, kinetic sculpture, pop art, Beat poetry, *haute couture*, comics, billboards, and French television. In examining the various aesthetic and cultural issues provoked by Klein's filmmaking, this chapter also suggests a correspondence between his work and Roland Barthes's intellectual project, a project that shares many of Klein's preoccupations, and even directly refers to his work when comparing photography to painted portraits.[5] How Klein has negotiated his identity as an American in Paris is also relevant to some of the book's broader contexts. Born into a downwardly mobile middle-class Jewish family in New York City, in 1928, Klein grew up on 108th Street and Amsterdam Avenue, near the Harlem end of Central Park. After the Second World War and a stint in the army, he availed himself of an ex-serviceman's educational grant and went to Paris to study art at the Sorbonne; and the city has remained his home ever since. Despite embracing this self-imposed exile, Klein has continued to film and photograph America, especially New York. Some of his most iconic street photographs were taken in the 1950s, in the streets of his childhood, and – as the chapter elucidates – much of his documentary filmmaking has involved expeditions into US culture in the second half of the twentieth century.

Both the chapters on Van der Keuken and Klein inevitably consider the significance of the 1960s, and 1968 in particular, on the development of their political views, and how the complexities of that era influenced their approach to film. Chapter 5 focuses on the work of Godard during 1968, and examines his interest in the radical potential of a new alliance or cultural front involving cinema and other contemporary popular forms. Godard's cinema typically foregrounds the rhetorical, fictionalising operations at work in any documentary project, and his broader preoccupations with the connections between film, photography, and the visual arts are reflected in his method: 'From the beginning', according to Peter Wollen, '[he] has shown a profound and yet paradoxical attachment to the traditions of European art, both as a heritage of great works and, at the same time, as an anarchic project which inevitably threatens every kind of tradition and norm'.[6] In exploring his work throughout 1968, this chapter focuses on a period in his career when he was disassociating himself from the post-war *auteur* tradition – a period not especially conducive to canonicity – as the end-titles to *Week-end* had famously declared a year earlier: 'Fin de conte – Fin de cinéma – Fin'.

Despite his political activism in 1968, Godard continued working on his film projects – most notably: *One Plus One*; the *Ciné-tracts* (or *Film-tracts*) project; and his ill-fated collaboration with D. A. Pennebaker and Richard Leacock, *One AM (One American Movie)*. These projects are characterised by a series of investigations into, and subversions of, the conventions of the documentary, especially in relation to television journalism and news coverage, where an increasingly stylised form of reportage-style realism doubly articulated the mass media's antagonism towards the cause of the students, strikers, and activists. Godard's work from this period is also characterised by a film language that incorporates forms derived from other visual art practices, especially painting, photography, graffiti and graphic art. Throughout the latter part of 1968, Godard dedicated time to the Dziga-Vertov Group (DVG), and – as he became further disillusioned with radical politics in France – he began to view the US as more fertile ground for revolution. Like Klein, Godard's imagination is always peculiarly alert to the complex historical and creative relations between France and the US, Europe and Hollywood.

The penultimate chapter in the book also picks up on this Euro-American theme in its discussion of two documentary treatments of the Central Park vigil for John Lennon, in December 1980: Jonas Mekas's *Happy Birthday to John* (1995, 16 mm, 18 min.), and Raymond Depardon's *Dix minutes de silence pour John Lennon/Ten Minutes Silence for John Lennon*

(1980, 16 mm, 10 min.). Mekas and Depardon might seem an unlikely pairing but as the chapter argues Lennon's death is not their only point of convergence: both their sensibilities have been shaped by migrant experiences, and much of their work, for all its formal differences, is preoccupied with exile and displacement, rootedness and the meaning of home; the country and the city (and in Mekas's case, the country in the city); both are Europeans who have developed an intimate social and creative relationship with New York City; both are concerned with the place of autobiography in their work, using captions, inter-titles, diary entries, still images, and first-person commentary to complicate relations between the imaginary and the documentary. What is also interesting is not simply differences in why and how these filmmakers witness the apotheosis of Lennon as cultural martyr (and naturalised New Yorker) but also how the phenomenon of public mourning displaces its ostensible subject: associatively, in the case of Mekas; incidentally, in the case of Depardon; and intentionally, in the case of the mass media.

Regarding the Real concludes with a discussion of Hiroshi Teshigahara's documentaries, especially his 1984 film, *Antonio Gaudí* (JP, 72 min.), examining how that film elucidates instances of convergence between documentary and architecture, as well as the more particular, and sometimes surprising, aesthetic correspondence between Teshigahara's visual style and that of Gaudí, Japanese *ikebana* (floral art) and Catalan *modernisme*. Cultural differences between New York and Paris or Amsterdam and London might pale into insignificance by comparison with those between Barcelona and Tokyo – especially, as there is no history of any meaningful economic relationship between Catalonia and Japan. There can, however, be little doubt that the Art Nouveau movement, and *Japonisme* in particular, influenced the arts in Catalonia. For example, Japan participated in both of the Barcelona Universal Expositions or 'Expos' in 1888 and 1929, and *Japonisme* influenced everything from the city's textile industry to its production of erotic art, and the orientalism of pioneer filmmaker, Segundo de Chomón.[7] Meanwhile, Gaudí's work has long been a source of fascination for Japanese intellectuals, especially among architects such as Kenji Imai, Hiroya Tanaka, Toshiaki Tange, and Tokutoshi Torii (who has written extensively on Gaudí), sculptors (for example, Etsuro Sotoo), or the photographer, Eikoh Hosoe, whose book, *Gaudí/Gaudí no uchu* was first published in 1984.[8] Sōfū Teshigahara, the father of Hiroshi, was particularly enthralled by Barcelona. A master (*iemoto*) of *ikebana*, Sōfū was an important figure in post-war Japanese cultural life, having established the Sōgetsu School of Ikebana in 1929. His approach to *ikebana* was radical, and although it remained fundamentally faithful to many of the traditions associated with Japanese floral art, it was also influenced by his travels through Europe in the 1930s, and his interest in surrealism. After the Second World War, Sōfū developed a strong connection with Catalan art and culture, and he became friends with Joan Miró, Antoni Tàpies, and Salvador Dalí (who appears with him in sequences from Hiroshi's early documentary shorts, *Ikebana* (1956, JP, 32 min.), and *Gaudí, Catalunya, 1959* (2008 [1959], JP, 16 mm, 19 min.)).

Although Hiroshi Teshigahara's *Woman in the Dunes/Sunna no onna* (1964, b&w, JP, 164 min.) secured his international reputation as a major figure of the Japanese New Wave, filmmaking only constituted one facet of his artistic activities, and – true to the Sōgetsu tradition – he was also an accomplished sculptor, ceramist, calligrapher, and landscape designer. He constructed large-scale bamboo installations, some of which clearly evoke the distinctive undulations and unruly geometry of Gaudí's architectural style. In making a film devoted to Gaudí's work, Teshigahara was also making a documentary about his own work and sensibility, and the influence of his father, who had died in 1979. In this sense, *Antonio Gaudí* is, perhaps, best seen as a companion to *Ikebana*, and an account of a legacy that is simultaneously intimate and distant, obvious and enigmatic. In its cinematography, subtle editing, and subdued soundtrack (composed by Tōru Takemitsu), *Antonio Gaudí* draws the spectator into its images and the histories those images signify, rather than the stories they may, or may not, exemplify.

Notes

1 Jean-Luc Godard, *Godard on Godard: Critical Writings*, eds Jean
   Narboni and Tom Milne (New York: Da Capo Press, 1986), p. 132.
2 Peter Wollen, *Paris Hollywood: Writings on Film* (London: Verso,
   2002), pp. 90–1.
3 For a comprehensive critical bibliography in this field, see
   Christine Sprengler's 'Cinema and the Visual Arts', in *Oxford
   Bibliographies* (Oxford: Oxford University Press), www.oxford-
   bibliographies.com/view/document/obo-9780199791286/obo-9780
   199791286-0122.xml [accessed 17/09/2013]. Two recent examples
   of studies that explore the integration of cinematic and pictorial
   techniques within an art documentary context are: Steven Jacobs,
   Framing Pictures: Film and the Visual Arts (Edinburgh: Edinburgh
   University Press, 2011), pp. 1–37; and Sally Shafto, 'Artistic
   Encounters: Jean-Marie Straub, Danièle Huillet, and Cézanne',
   in *Film, Art, New Media: Museum without Walls?* ed., Angela Dalle
   Vacche (Basingstoke: Palgrave Macmillan, 2012), pp. 199–220. See
   also: *Framing Film: Cinema and the Visual Arts*, eds Steven Allen
   and Laura Hubner (Bristol: Intellect, 2012); Susan Felleman's
   Real Objects in Unreal Situations: Modern Art in Fiction Films
   (Bristol: Intellect, 2014), and *The Image in Dispute: Art and Cinema
   in the Age of Photography*, ed. Dudley Andrew (Austin: University
   of Texas Press, 1997).
4 Bill Nichols, 'Documentary Film and the Modernist Avant-
   Garde', *Critical Inquiry*, 27.4 (2001), p. 582.
5 Qtd. in Roger Horrocks, *Len Lye: A Biography* (Auckland:
   University of Auckland Press, 2002), p. 148.
6 Roland Barthes, *Camera Lucida: Reflections on Photography*, trans.
   Richard Howard (London: Jonathan Cape, 1982), pp. 28–30, 46–7.
7 Writings – and curatorial work – by contemporary Catalan art his-
   torians such as Fernando García Gutiérrez, Elena Barlés Báguena,
   V. David Almazán Tomás, and Richard Bru has shed much light
   on the influence of *Japonisme* on art in Catalonia. See Gutiérrez *et
   al.* eds, *Arte japonés y japonismo*. Ex. cat. (Bilbao: Bilbao Fine Arts
   Museum, 2014).
8 For example, in August 1939, the Tokyo-based journal, *Kentiku
   Sekai: Japanese Journal of Building and Living Culture* published Kenji Imai's 'Architecture of Barcelona: Sagrada Familia
   Cathedral'. Both volumes of Tokutoshi Torii's *El mundo enigmático
   de Gaudí* were published in 1983 (Madrid: Instituto de España),

while Eikoh Hosoe's *Gaudí/Gaudí no uchu* (Tokyo: Shueisha) became the basis for subsequent international exhibitions and catalogues devoted to Hosoe's 'Gaudí photographs'. On the influence of modernist cinema on Teshigahara, see Felicy Gee's 'Surrealist Legacies: The Influence of Luis Buñuel's "Irrationality" on Hiroshi Teshigahara's Documentary-Fantasy', in *A Companion to Luis Buñuel*, eds Rob Stone and Julian Gutierrez-Albilla (Oxford: Wiley-Blackwell, 2013), pp. 572–89.

1

Suspended animation

I'm a film-thinker, otherwise uncultured. (Len Lye)[1]

The GPO Film Unit is the most iconic of the various state-sponsored and independent organisations that comprised the British Documentary Movement of the inter-war period. Its outline history tends to go as follows: in the middle of economic recession, social unrest, and the spread of fascism, Stephen Tallents and John Grierson salvaged a dedicated public-service film unit from the recently defunct Empire Marketing Board (EMB). Funded through the General Post Office, the unit existed from 1933–39, with an ostensible brief to produce short films promoting the work of government departments, and informing the public about the condition of Britain. Throughout most of this period, Grierson nurtured a diverse group of filmmakers, and he came to regard his time there as the moment when documentary filmmaking entered 'the field of social problems, and keyed it to the task of describing not only industrial and commercial spectacle but social truth as well'. Thereafter, classic GPO films, such as *Post Haste* (Humphrey Jennings, 1934, 26 min.), *Weather Forecast* (Evelyn Cherry, 1934, 20 min.), *Housing Problems* (Arthur Elton and Edgar Anstey, 1935, 13 min.), *The King's Stamp* (William Coldstream, 1935, 20 min.), and *Night Mail* (Basil Wright and Harry Watt, 1936, 24 min.) became associated with the representation of this treatment of 'social truth', and with a notion of the documentary film as showing 'the common man, not in the romance of his calling, but in the more complex and intimate drama of his citizenship'.[2]

In simplifying into sociology the artistic environment that

produced the GPO (and EMB) films of the late 1920s and 1930s, however, Grierson also strategically distanced this body of work from the reactions *against* realism still being felt throughout the culture of modernism, especially in the fields of painting, design, sculpture, literature, and music: the films of Wright, Jennings, and Coldstream owe as much to the remnants of European surrealism as to the tenets of Griersonian realism. Len Lye, in particular, experimented across a wide range of art forms, conscientiously avoiding too direct an association with any given film genre, movement or manifesto, working *from* groups rather than *for* them. His involvement with Grierson and the GPO throughout the 1930s was an important chapter in a career characterised by a defiant – anarchic, even – attitude towards authorities and institutions. Not surprisingly, his GPO films – namely, *A Colour Box* (1935, 4 min.), *Rainbow Dance* (1936, 5 min.), *Trade Tattoo* (1937, 5 min.), and *N. or N.W.* (1937, 7 min.) – have been rendered incidental to histories of the Documentary Movement during the 1930s. Like the GPO films of Norman McLaren and Lotte Reiniger from this period, however, Lye's work is integral to any comprehensive assessment of this movement and its relations to a wider visual culture, relations that contributed to its success in extending the scope of documentary film language.

Travels/doodles

Lye was born in Christchurch, New Zealand on 5 July 1901. His parents were poor first-generation immigrants: Irish Catholic on his mother's side and English Protestant on his father's. Like Stan Brakhage in the 1950s, Lye's discovery of Ezra Pound's 1916 essay-memoir of Henri Gaudier-Brzeska proved revelatory and he was soon attracted to the artworks of the European modernists, principally, those associated with Constructivism, Futurism, Vorticism, and Cubism. Lye's engagement with surrealism emerged later and would become relevant to his work throughout the 1930s. His interest in tribal art and cultures, and the instinctual creativity of the body, intensified after he read more widely on aspects of comparative mythology, dance rituals, and fertility symbolism – reading Freud's *Totem and Taboo* (1913) was a particularly illuminating experience for him. In 1922, he moved to Sydney where he secured some work with an advertising company specialising in the production of short commercial films. This direct contact with work-a-day filmmakers and the raw materials of their craft convinced him that film – especially the animated film – was an ideal medium to explore the practical applications of his own evolving kinaesthetic theories. (It may also have given him knowledge of early film advertising techniques and tricks that would prove useful when he started working at the GPO.) After spending nearly two years in western Samoa, Lye returned briefly to Australia before heading to England in 1926.

The cultural milieu in London at this time was receptive to Lye's methods and outlook, and he immediately set to work producing new paintings, batiks, and small sculptures. Lye's friend from Sydney, the Australian composer Jack Ellitt, also migrated to London at this time, and they began collaborating on what would be Lye's first short film, *Tusalava* (1929, silent, 10 min.) – an animation based on Aboriginal myths of the witchetty grub. His work began to attract admirers and he struck up relations with numerous artists and writers, including Coldstream, Jennings, Eric Kennington, Norman Cameron, Ben Nicholson, Laurie Lee, Oswell Blakeston, Laura Riding, and Robert Graves. One of his first commissions involved designing title page symbols for Seizin Press, Graves's and Riding's small (Majorca-based) publishing company. He effectively became the artist-in-residence at Seizin, drawing the motifs and designing the covers for several books, including Riding's *Love as Death, Death as Death* (1928), and a new edition of Gertrude Stein's *An Acquaintance with Description* (1929). With Riding's editorial assistance, he completed his first book, *No Trouble* (1930), a collection of letters also published by Seizin. These commissions were important, securing for Lye a creative home relatively free from the distractions of institutional pressures, and institutional personalities. At the same time, the formation of the London Film Society in

1925 also assisted Lye's career. Although the Film Society was originally founded with the principal aim of exhibiting modernist cinema, its membership was intellectually diverse. This was reflected in its programmes, which included a variety of British as well as European and Soviet films. In addition to enjoying the active support of Fabians like H. G. Wells, George Bernard Shaw, and J. M. Keynes, the society also comprised filmmakers and visual artists. Grierson and Thorold Dickinson were among those who endorsed its support for new exhibition quotas in Britain, while abstract artists such as Nicholson and Frank Dobson viewed the Society as a natural ally in their struggles against the academic predilections of the British art establishment. Lye joined the Society in 1928, and was given the opportunity to see important modern films, and meet visiting filmmakers, including Hans Richter (who impressed him) and Sergei Eisenstein (who didn't). The Film Society, for its part, was excited by Lye's novel approach to animation, and it agreed to provide him with sufficient funding to complete *Tusalava*, which was screened as part of the Film Society's 33rd programme, in December 1929.

One of the Society's co-founders, Sidney Bernstein, also went on to sponsor Lye's next film – a three-minute puppet film entitled *Experimental Animation* (aka *Peanut Vendor*) (1934, 3 min.). During this period, Lye's interest in 'colour music' and the free-hand soundtrack is similar to the audiovisual experiments of László Moholy-Nagy, and Viking Eggeling. Coincidentally, Moholy-Nagy lived and worked with other Bauhaus artists in London between 1935 and 1937, and the parallels between his career at this time and that of Lye are striking: while in England, Moholy-Nagy attended screenings of GPO films, began painting on transparent plastics, received a major advertising commission from Imperial Airways, and was involved in several documentary film projects; footage from his *Play of Light Black–White–Grey/Ein Lichtspiel Schwarz–weiss–grau* (1930, 6 min.), for example, was included at the beginning of Stuart Legg's GPO film, *The Coming of the Dial* (1933, 14 min.).[3] Meanwhile, Nicholson's *coup* at the Seven and Five Society was another event that would – inadvertently

– assist Lye's career. The Seven and Five Society was originally formed in 1919 to exhibit non-modernist British art
but by the late 1920s it had become the primary exhibitor of
abstract art in Britain. Nicholson, who had joined the Society
in 1924, spearheaded this fundamental change in the Society's
exhibition policy. In 1927, Nicholson invited Lye to be a guest
exhibitor in the Society's January exhibition, and this experience brought Lye into contact with artists associated with surrealism, including Jennings, who had just returned from Paris,
and Alberto Cavalcanti, whose surrealist 'city symphony',
Nothing But Time/Rien que les heures (1926, silent, 45 min.) was
also screened by the Film Society in 1929, and who would
subsequently introduce both Lye and Jennings (separately) to
Grierson, and work with them at the GPO Film Unit. By the
early 1930s, however, Lye had become disappointed at how
Nicholson and the Seven and Five Society (renamed the Seven
and Five Abstract Group in 1935) were developing their purer
notion of abstract art, and he initially reacted against this by
aligning himself more closely to surrealism: 'Like Riding in
her *Histories*, Lye produced much of his work in the 1930s in
dialogue with surrealism – he admired Miró, and wrote prose
pieces in an "automatic" style indebted to Breton and Stein …
[he] exhibited paintings at the London Surrealist exhibitions
of 1936 and 1937, and practised automatic doodling.'[4]

While Lye had made a name for himself as an abstract
painter and print designer, his career as a filmmaker had fal-
tered after the modest success of *Tusalava*. The *Experimental
Animation* project had provided him with some useful technical experience but it was followed by a number of failures,
and finding the financial and technical resources to make new
animated films was proving impossible. It was at this point he
decided to revive some of his Australian 'scratch' experiments:
using discarded film leaders, he had started trying to synchronise the movement of scratches and marks on the celluloid
with different musical sequences. Developing his handmade
technique, he now began painting directly on transparent
and processed film stock, using coloured lacquers and mis-
cellaneous instruments (brushes, bones, combs, stencils, etc.).

When projected, Lye's (un-photographed) film images yielded up a vivid array of colours, textures, shapes, and rhythms.[5] Crucially, he also quickly developed an effective printmaking technique for his footage and in so doing earned a place for himself alongside the other major contemporary innovators in the field of animation: namely, Oskar Fischinger, Berthold Bartosch, Alexandre Alexeïeff, Walt Disney, McLaren, and Reiniger – who made several short silhouette films at the GPO, including *The Heavenly Post Office* (1938, col. 4 min.) and *The Tocher* (1938, b&w, 5 min.). For Lye, meanwhile, this direct method of filmmaking had another attribute: it was cheap. No cameras were required and post-production editing was minimal. In freeing the artist from the responsibilities of concrete figuration and geometric precision, the images could be created automatically, flowing more readily from the primitive energies of the Old Brain (Lye's preferred term for the unconscious), rather than from the logical (realist) processes of the 'New Brain'.

Lye's concept of an Old Brain (and its variants) remained central to his understanding of the relationship between primordial instincts and creative expression. Since his time in Australia and western Samoa in the 1920s, he had been trying to develop an artistic practice that circumvented rationality and responded directly to the rhythms of the body, and the images of the unconscious. While there are similarities between this approach and surrealism's privileging of the body and the unconscious, Lye's kinaesthetic attitude was much more anti-rational, anarchic, and a-political. Although, as Michel Remy has pointed out, *Tusalava* 'shows affinities with surrealist qualities apparent in the works of Joan Miró, Paul Klee or Desmond Morris' and his 'exploration of "doodles" ... links up with the surrealist theory of automatism', Lye had become sceptical about surrealism, seeing too much 'new brain' ingenuity in its paintings, films, and manifestos.[6] Writing in 1937, he remarked:

> The surreals have yet to cotton that their good emphasis on the mind stuff is sifted through the old mind enemy living real-

ity eye-check sieve. Hearts in the right place: minds hinged on polarities for mind catching interest: twisting the reality set-up. Showing the mind in whimsical dream ticktock. A Hi! Hi! and three ticks off the dead lamb's tail with a living emphasis swish.[7]

Arguably, Lye's appropriation of primitive forms and direct techniques is also more playful and sympathetic than that of painters such as Adolph Gottlieb, Jackson Pollock, and Willem de Kooning. Lye's aesthetic ambitions were unsophisticated: motion, sounds, images, and sensations. As he later commented: 'The whole business with any art is first, *empathy*; then a good aesthetic level of imagery; and finally, getting and keeping the vicarious evocations of the imagery going.'[8] It was the principle of 'keeping things going', and gaining access to Old Brain energies that explains his initial engagement with – and subsequent estrangement from – surrealism in the 1930s, abstract expressionism in the 1950s, and the Kinetic Art Movement in the 1960s.

Actuality/whimsicality

Lye's commitment to abstract imagery rather than social reality is not something normally associated with the film unit Grierson had inaugurated at the EMB, and which he then consolidated during his four-year stint as Film Officer at the GPO. Indeed, shortly before his first commission from the Unit, Lye (and Laura Riding) had declared that the cinema 'cannot visualize meaning – meaning, or explanatory sense is not visualizable'.[9] This notion (and the entire tenor of their 1935 statement on filmmaking) is – if anything – antithetical to Grierson's description of the origins and aims of *his* school of film: 'It is worth recalling that the British documentary group began not much in affection for film per se as in affection for national education. If I am to be counted as the founder and leader of the movement, its origins certainly lay in sociological rather than aesthetic aims.'[10] While Grierson's recollection is accurate in one sense, his attitude to 'film *per se*' and 'aesthetic aims' was more ambivalent than such pronouncements suggest. After he left the GPO in 1937, for example, Grierson continued to emphasise the educational achievements of the Unit, divorcing it from the influence of modernist visual and literary culture – although it is probably also true that he became 'strongly influenced by the didactic style of *March of Time* during the late 1930s, and Paul Rotha has claimed this had an undue influence on his ideas'.[11] Yet, key appointments to the GPO Film Unit (most notably, Ivor Montagu, Wright, Anstey, and especially, Coldstream, Cavalcanti, and Jennings) had worked extensively within and across avant-garde movements in the 1920s. Indeed, so had Grierson himself, both through his active involvement in the Film Society, and his own EMB film, *Drifters* (1929, 61 min.), a film that – as Jamie Sexton puts it – was 'abstract documentary that employed "uniquely cinematic" strategies, followed international modernist filmmaking precedents, and was heavily influenced by machine aesthetics'.[12] Even his later short, *Granton Trawler* (1934, 11 min.), although a realistic depiction of the hardships of trawler fishing, is strongly influenced by Soviet montage techniques, and its soundtrack (created by Cavalcanti) owes much to contemporary modernist experiments with sound–image a-synchronicity. In a discussion of the converging practices of avant-garde and documentary filmmakers in Britain during the 1920s and 1930s, Michael O'Pray surmises: 'Grierson's own suspicion of aestheticism in film is undermined in *Granton Trawler*, perhaps suggesting that what he feared most was his own artistic proclivities and not so much those of others.'[13]

Under film units such as EMB, GPO, and Realist (all associated with Grierson) British film culture in the 1930s had become synonymous with a socially informed and distinctive documentary practice. As indicated above, the contradictory nature of this 'movement' – and the diversity of artistic activities and international influences it contained – still tends to be overshadowed by eulogies to Grierson's theory of the democratic documentary, the perceived need to canonise a realist documentary tradition, and resolve once and for all what Grierson meant by his on-the-hoof definition of documentary film as the 'creative treatment of actuality'. Despite his posturing, and in the face of hostile lobbying from the film trade and scrutiny from various parliamentary committees, Grierson and Tallents did skilfully defend the funding of the Unit by strategically downplaying the actual scope of its aesthetic innovations. However, while Grierson's pragmatism at the GPO was legendary it is also important to bear in mind that it would have been impossible had he ever harboured a genuinely radical social vision to begin with. Although compromised by the corporatist ethics of public and private sponsorship, his views on informed citizenship, social reform, and state intervention were consistent with broadly progressive political opinion at that time. Suffice to say, Grierson's ideological project at the EMB and GPO film units was culturally ambitious but never politically radical: it involved facilitating the production of state-funded promotional and educational films, offering audiences an alternative to the Hollywood and British features that had become the staple of British cinema audiences since the mid 1920s. Grierson's new type of documentary was to be propagandistic, in the soft sense, i.e. it would function as a source of civic enlightenment, educating the public at large about social conditions, and promoting state services. From his EMB days, Grierson also maintained the conviction that the publicly funded documentary film ought to disseminate news from elsewhere, particularly when it functioned to showcase images from the outer reaches of Britain's expiring empire (as in a film such as Basil Wrights's *Song of Ceylon* (1934, 38 min.).

Grierson's recruitment of Lye to the GPO offers an insight into his complicated attitude to the relations between entertainment and propaganda, artistic experimentation and mass communication, an attitude that – between 1935 and 1938 – created a space for Lye's formal whimsicality and 'affection for film' within a unit that was to be directly (or indirectly) involved in the production of virtually all of Lye's 35 mm. films. In early 1935, Lye and Ellitt collaborated with John Gielgud on *Full Fathom Five*, a short animated film inspired by Ariel's speech in *The Tempest*: 'Once [Gielgud's] reading was recorded on film, Ellitt measured the phrases for Lye who then painted designs directly onto the same film strip.'[14] On the advice of

Cavalcanti, Lye took the film to Grierson, who watched it and then offered to buy it on condition a GPO advertising slogan was added to the film at the end. On the evidence of *Full Fathom Five*, it was clear Lye was an innovator capable of producing engaging, witty films possessing none of the severe formalism characteristic of animated films associated with the European avant-garde of the time. While Grierson was hardly going to be in thrall to Lye's kinaesthetic practices, Old Brain theories, and de facto rejection of Enlightenment thinking, he was impressed by the artisan (handmade) quality of Lye's creative techniques, techniques that further demonstrated for Grierson the viability of working successfully outside a highly regulated and expensive studio system. While a film such as *Full Fathom Five* would make little practical contribution to the GPO Film Unit's promotional remit, it did embody the spirit of a spontaneous, modern film that owed nothing to the sterile, screenplay-orientated production culture being denounced by Grierson and others at that time. Furthermore, Lye's experiments with colour and music had an added commercial appeal: his films would 'liven up the GPO Unit's packages of black-and-white documentaries'. In Lye, the Unit had found for itself 'a wonderful odd ball', as Grierson called him on one occasion, and 'essentially a *flâneur* … a tinkerer', as he described him on another – comments which say more about Grierson's prejudices than Lye idiosyncrasies.[15]

During his time at the GPO Unit, Lye completed nine short films, including a new version of *Full Fathom Five* (1937, 9 min.). The Unit directly produced four of these films: *A Colour Box* (prod. Grierson); *Rainbow Dance* (prod. Wright and Cavalcanti); *Trade Tattoo* (prod. Grierson); and *N. or N.W.* (prod. Cavalcanti). With the exception of *N. or N.W.*, all of Lye's films from this period were animated colour films using music either composed or arranged by Ellitt. Lye experimented across the full range of available colour processes: Dufaycolor for *A Colour Box* and *Kaleidoscope*; Gasparcolor for *The Birth of the Robot* and *Rainbow Dance*; and Technicolor for *Trade Tattoo*. *Kaleidoscope* (1935, prod. Noxon, Imperial Tobacco, 4 min.) and *The Birth of the Robot* (1936, prod. Jennings, Shell-

Mex and BP Ltd, 7 min.) were funded by corporate sponsors, although the small production teams for both films were
mainly GPO Film Unit staff. Lye's filmography from the 1930s
reveals much about the penumbra of production modes and
distribution arrangements surrounding the GPO, and other
film units during the inter-war period. While Lye – for the
most part – remained detached from political engagement,
his GPO animated films and one 'live action' short are still
relevant to an understanding of the British Documentary
Movement. His work from the 1930s, like those of Norman
McLaren in the 1940s, can too easily be dismissed as novel
exercises in advertising art and the public information or promotional film, rather than films that are also interrogating and
subverting attempts to institutionalise documentary practices,
and contain them with rigidly generic categories. Ironically,
many of the GPO films from the Grierson era were themselves
experimental, and all were promotional, even when they were
promoting the documentary achievements of the Unit itself.
Lye's work at the GPO still reveals the very contingent nature
of the distinctions habitually invoked in relation to this era in
the history of the documentary film (i.e. realism/abstraction,
documentary/avant-garde, propagandistic/promotional, etc.)
offering alternative perspectives on a more complex – and certainly, more modern – British film culture of the 1930s than
the one constructed by Grierson in his subsequent writings,
and rhetoric.

Boxes/letters

Lye's commitment to a modernist rendering of animation
and documentary forms is apparent, for example, in his deft
integration of corporate advertising captions and slogans into
each of his GPO films. For example, *A Colour Box* informs
its audiences about the price of parcel postage (communication and convenience); *Rainbow Dance* extols the benefits
of a Post Office savings account (banking and leisure); and
Trade Tattoo celebrates 'the rhythm of work-a-day Britain'
(industry and commerce). In each case, Lye avoids giving any

sense that the captions were added as a post-production after-thought. Stencilled letters, silhouettes, numbers, words, and symbols flow into the filmic realm and assemble themselves into legibility in a manner consistent with the overall visual and rhythmical shape, and soundscape, of each film. Lye's graphic inventiveness is also apparent in the frequent super-imposition of abstract colours and moving shapes onto found footage, footage consisting entirely of leftover material from other GPO films. In *Rainbow Dance*, for example, simple sten-cilled images of fish and boats are superimposed on to translu-cently rendered footage of various seascapes, while a bright red cut-out of a toy train chugs across an Ordnance Survey map. A tennis match, performed by the film's silhouetted dancer, Rupert Doone – who had recently co-founded London's Group Theatre – is discernible amid floating shapes and vivid colour combinations; on two occasions during this sequence, cuts are made to a spectator, and this repeated shot comprises a neg-ative, solarised, image (anticipating Reiniger). Although Lye used a different colour process for each film, both the Gaspar colour process (*Rainbow Dance*) and Technicolor (*Trade Tattoo*) allowed for a greater degree of colour separation and re-synthesis than the Dufay system which 'had a tendency to produce soft, de-saturated colours which did not always suit [Lye's] bold effects'.[16] Typically, Lye did not just apply colour processes; he experimented freely with each process, inventing countless new chromatic effects. While his experiments with colour mixing and masking were influenced by the attempts of other more experimental filmmakers to map colour (and sonic) formations onto psychic states, they are also distinctive in that Lye was attempting to reactivate Old Brain mechanisms through the experience of creating and projecting unusual con-trasts of tone and texture. His direct technique becomes less pronounced across his trilogy of GPO animated films, but it is always present, acting as a striking and abstract corrective to a more realistic arrangement of animated and documen-tary images. These films – even with their increasing tendency towards a greater level of figurative representation – generate a productive tension between the textural looseness of random shapes and colourscapes on the one hand, and the compositional determinants of the frame on the other. In each case, the accompanying dance music accentuates the free choreography of Lye's doodles, free lines, brush strokes, superimpositions, stencils, and stamp prints.

This playful synchronicity of sound and image enables Lye's films to key into bodily rather than psychological states, an assumption consistent with his more general celebration of free movement: figures of motion rather than motivated figuration. At one level, Lye's interest in improvisational jazz and scat music (e.g. *Musical Poster # 1* (1940, 3 min.) and *Tal Farlow* (1980, 1.5 min.)) is foreshadowed in the music chosen and edited for *A Colour Box*, *Rainbow Dance*, and *Trade Tattoo* (as well as *Kaleidoscope*). For *A Colour Box* and *Kaleidoscope*, for example, Lye and Ellitt used recordings of Biguine variations performed by Emilio 'Don' Barreto and his Cuban Orchestra. Barreto and his band of Cuban expatriates had earned notoriety in the late 1920s when they brought the rumba to the nightclubs of Paris and the French Riviera. Barreto's fusion of 1920s swing melodies with Afro-Cuban rhythms, like the Latino-style composition used in *Rainbow Dance* ('Tony's Wife', performed by Rico's Creole Band), coincided with Lye's own attempts to generate images that shimmied and swooned (syncopated) with the music. In *N. or N.W.*, the sense of objects and objectives flowing freely and easily away from the plot of the film is conveyed throughout by Jazz tunes that alternatively accompany and contradict narrative moods, decisions, actions: 'I'm Gonna Sit Right Down' (Fats Waller), 'T'aint No Use' (Benny Goodman), and 'Give Me a Break' (Bob Howard).

What appealed to Lye and Ellitt about this style of music – and the African and West Indies music Lye used in his 1950s New York films – was its physicality, the blurring of distinctions between dance and music, performing and listening, activity and contemplation. True to his primitivist inclinations, Lye believed in an intimate connection between the act of filmmaking and the performance of dance. As Ian Christie, for example, explains: 'These are "dance films" without dancers, where the image itself dances, with the primary elements of mark-making – lines, points, patterns – moving in rhythmic patterns to the dance soundtrack, and suggesting, as Lye wrote in 1936, a "sensory ballet".[17] Through primitivism, dance had influenced a wide range of modernist forms and practices, particularly painting (e.g. Picasso and Matisse), sculpture (e.g. Rodin and Epstein), theatre (e.g. Meyerhold and Craig) and, of course, the cinema: the dancing of Gene Kelly owes as much to Jazz and Nijinsky as it does to *Broadway Melody* and Busby Berkeley. In Lye's case, dance was integral to his broader notion of primordial rhythms, and to attuning the body to the rhythms of the Old Brain. Hence, the animated image in *A Colour Box*, *Rainbow Dance*, and *Trade Tattoo* does more than merely accompany or react to the music. If anything, what the films achieve is a more disruptive relationship between visual images and aural rhythms. In the gap between a sound and the movement of an image, there exists a moment of imperfect simultaneity, and Lye was clearly fascinated by how film (like dance, and motion sculpture) can never completely conceal the moment of its own paradox, the fact of its own fictionality.

Although, strictly speaking, a live-action – rather than an animated – documentary film, *N. or N.W.* also exploits this paradox, transcending its informational, promotional rationale with a carefully arranged array of abstract figurations. In narrative terms, the film dramatises a suburban romantic vignette to illustrate the importance of correct postcode usage, and, *a fortiori*, the resourcefulness and reliability of the British postal service. The film's shot structures and elliptical montage techniques, surreal associations and jokes, combine to subordinate its documentary rationale and thematic core to an alternative set of cinematic and hermeneutic possibilities: the real message – that there really is no message – is in the *mise en scène*. The film opens with an extreme low-angle close shot of a young woman's (Evelyn) face and hand. She is holding a pen, trying to write a letter to her lover (Jack) but is distracted by memories of their argument (about Jack's jealous behaviour) the previous evening. The film then cuts to another close-up, this time of the writing paper where 'Dear Jack' and 'I don't know why …' have been scored out. There then follows a dream-like shot of the letter being held up like a mask in front of Evelyn's face – an oval-shaped hole has been cut out where her mouth is. The camera angle changes again as Evelyn faces us squarely in a tight medium close shot, full of renewed determination: the weekend in the country is cancelled. The film then cuts to Jack, pacing around his darkened study thinking of Evelyn's 'marvellous dark eyes' (at which point the camera cuts mischievously to a close shot showing the *Orient Blue* writing pad on his desk). Jack switches on the light and resolves to write a letter of apology and the film again cuts to another shot of a face behind a letter with a section of the letter/mask cut out (for Jack's nose, this time). Jack writes hastily but then hesitates over the postcode: 'N. or N.W.1?'. He makes what turns out to be the wrong choice (N.W.1). Once posted, his letter is delayed and Evelyn – unaware of Jack's apology – assumes the worst and writes a final letter (of *resignation*), enclosing her engagement ring. Suddenly, there is a knock at the door, Evelyn rushes out and is handed Jack's errant letter by a burly postman. All's well that ends well: Evelyn tears up her letter, and slips the ring back on. The film ends with shots of Jack and Evelyn swimming in a lake, teasing one another, and feeding swans. As they lie sunbathing on the grass, Jack arranges leaves on Evelyn's leg to protect her skin from the sun: 'Just like babes in the wood?', she asks.

In *N. or N.W.*, Lye takes a rudimentary, promotional scenario and transforms it into a cinematic *jeu d'espirt*. Distorted low and high-angle angle shots, sudden close-ups, jump cuts, silhouettes, superimposed negative and overexposed images are used throughout the letter-writing sequences to register the protagonists' desires and anxieties. Yet, if the film is about anything (other than postcodes), it is about writing itself: intentional and automatic, formal and formless. Its 'chalk on glass' animated sequences, for example, invoke Freud's 1925 essay 'A Note Upon the "Mystic Writing Pad"', Lye's interest in psychoanalytical methods (why did Jack *really* get the code wrong?), and also his own 'scratch' experiments and direct filmmaking techniques: 'If we imagine one hand writing upon the surface of the Mystic Writing Pad while another periodically raises

1   *N. or N.W.*

its covering sheet from the wax slab, we shall have a concrete
representation of the way in which I tried to picture the func-
tioning of the perceptual apparatus of our mind.'[18] The writing
sequences shot from underneath a glass screen also – as Kevin
Jackson and others have suggested – anticipate the Picasso
documentaries by Paul Haesaerts (*Visite à Picasso/Bezoek aan
Picasso*, 1950, Bel., b&w, 21 min.), and Henri-George Clouzot
(*The Picasso Mystery/Le Mystère Picasso*, 1956, col., 78 min.),
where a similar technique is used to film the artist at work.[19]
N. or N.W. is structured less around the actions and reactions
of its protagonists than by an elaborate system of graphic –
hieroglyphic – forms: letters (and letters from letters), animated dots and splotches, doodles, maps, drawings, 'leaves',
gestures. As the letters are being written, sent, and received
superimposed fragments of handwritten text accompany the
couple's airy voices and confused desires. This film's abstract
approach to the mundane world of letter-writing and the postage system may also owe something to the influence of Laura
Riding, who was fascinated by the epistolary genre. In 1935,

the same year in which she co-authored 'Film-Making' with
Lye, Riding edited four issues of the journal *Focus* (each one
a collection of letters), and in 1933 she completed *Everybody's
Letters* which comprised ninety-four actual posted letters by
various people (with only the names and addresses changed),
and 'a long "Editorial Postscript" that offers some of the most
sustained theorising of epistolarity ever written, most of it on
the universal or "true" letter'.[20]

Writing in the 1960s, Lye would justify his fusion of documentary, live-action, and animation techniques in *N. or N.W.*
in terms what he described as an attempt to 'get out of the
[D.W.] Griffith technique'. In other words, the modern artist
resists the suppression of a genuinely kinetic – primitive –
film aesthetic and the institutionalisation of realism: 'I was
interested in ... taking real live action in the studio under
circumstances in which your understanding of motion would
be such that you could break that motion right down and
build it up again in cinema terms, kinetic terms.'[21] In one
sequence – which was regrettably cut from the film, and then
lost – Lye even attempted 'to present a walk [in the manner
of Marcel Duchamp's 'Nude Descending a Staircase' (1912)]
by an abbreviated series of images or signs of walking'.[22] *N.
or N.W.* is another link between the GPO Film Unit and the
images and montages of René Magritte, Dalí and Buñuel, and
especially René Clair (and *Entr'acte* (1924, 22 min.), and Man
Ray). Once posted, Evelyn's and Jack's letters traverse through
a suburban Wonderland of flying postboxes, spinning road
maps, and cascading skies before arriving at their destinations.
For the surrealists the line between the actual and the mythical, the documentary and the imaginary, is not so much thin
as non-existent, and *N. or N.W.* remains a richly associative
and provocative example of modernist filmmaking: there are
few live-action documentary shorts from the 1930s that can
leave one pondering Freud and *le facteur*, postal artwork and
the Fluxus group, Laura Riding and Yoko Ono, Jacques Tati
and Gertrude Stein, the invention of email, text messaging,
teletheory, the demise of the handwritten letter.

After changes at the GPO Film Unit, including Grierson's

resignation in 1938, Lye looked for commercial film work to support his family, and to continue subsidising his music and colour animation experiments. Before accepting a more secure arrangement with Basil Wright's newly founded Realist Film Unit – which was now receiving regular commissions from the government to make wartime public information and propaganda films – Lye made *Colour Flight* (1938, Gasparcolour, 4 min.) for Imperial Airlines, and *Swinging the Lambeth Walk* (1939, Dufaycolour, 4 min.), for the Tourism and Industrial Development Association, and *Musical Poster #1* (1940, Technicolor, 3 min.), a 'poster film' produced for the Ministry of Information (with a mischievously ironic take on wartime paranoia). Even in the black-and-white films he made for Realist, especially the earlier works (such, as *When the Pie Was Opened* (1941, 8 min.) and *Newspaper Train* (1942, 7 min.)), Lye continued to explore the kinaesthetic aspects of film, combining animation with documentary and live-action sequences. In 1944, however, the offer of a sojourn in New York proved irresistible and once he had disentangled himself from other commitments in London, he accepted a commission from the producers of *The March of Time* to collaborate with I. A. Richards on a series of short documentaries on teaching Basic English. Settling into an apartment on Lexington Avenue (passed on to him by Jennings), Lye embraced New York as another centre of artistic innovation, and he was soon socialising in Greenwich Village, and 'The Club': 'New York is a fantastic merging of people, of all sorts, shapes, sizes and dispositions and what not ... in which you get the absolute worst and the absolute best.'[23] In leaving London for New York, Lye also returned to painting and poetry, as well as direct and scratch filmmaking techniques, and his reputation as an avant-garde filmmaker would be further consolidated throughout the 1950s with *Color Cry* (1953, 3 min.), *Free Radicals* (1958, b&w, 4 min.), and *Rhythm* (1957, b&w, 1 min.). The latter film was originally commissioned by the Chrysler Corporation to promote its latest Windsor sedan, and the corporation's slick assembly-line production methods. As P. Adams Sitney puts it: 'By radically reducing the film to a minute, in thousands of

2 *Rhythm*

jump cuts, Lye created ... an aptly titled work [that] affirms the priority of the twenty-four-beats-per-second pulse of cinema over the industrial pace of the assembly line.'[24] Needless to say, Chrysler preferred something different.

Notes

1   Len Lye, *Figures of Motion: Selected Writings*, eds Wystan Curnow and Roger Horrocks (Auckland: Auckland University Press, 1984), p. 103.

2   John Grierson, 'Battle for Authenticity [1933]', in *Grierson on Documentary*, ed. Forsyth Hardy (London: Faber, 1979), pp. 215–16.

3   Rachel Low, *The History of British Film*, vol. 2 (London: Routledge, 1997 [1950]), p. 81.

4   Tim Armstrong, 'Len Lye and Laura Riding in the 1930s: The Impossibility of Film and Literature', in *Literature and Visual Technologies: Writing After Cinema*, eds Julian Murphet and Lydia Rainford (Basingstoke: Palgrave Macmillan, 2003), p. 126.

5   'The direct application of paint to the surface of film transformed

the dynamics of the graphic film. Colour could be rendered more vivid than it could by the photographic process; the different kinds and densities of paint opened a range of texture hitherto ignored; and above all the problems of shape, scale, and the illusions of perspective which the early graphic filmmakers inherited from the painterly and photographic traditions could be bracketed by an imagery that remained flat on the plane of the screen and avoided geometric contour' (P. Adams Sitney, *Visionary Film: The American Avant-Garde: 1943–2000*, 3rd edn (New York: Oxford University Press, 2002), p. 233).

6   Michel Remy, *Surrealism in Britain* (Aldershot: Ashgate, 1999), pp. 55–7.

7   Lye, *Figures of Motion*, p. 118.

8   Lye, 'A Note on Film and Dance [1967]', *Figures of Motion*, p. 56.

9   Lye and Laura Riding, 'Film-Making [1935]', *Figures of Motion*, p. 40.

10 Grierson, 'The Course of Realism [1935]', *Grierson on Documentary*, p. 78.

11 Ian Aiken, *Film and Reform: John Grierson and the Documentary Film Movement* (London: Routledge, 1990), p. 144. Brian Winston, *Claiming the Real: The Griersonian Documentary and Its Legitimations*, 2nd edn (London: BFI, 2008), pp. 24–93.

12 Jamie Sexton, 'Grierson's Machines: *Drifters*, the Documentary Film Movement and the Negotiation of Modernity', *Canadian Journal of Film Studies*, 11.1 (2002), p. 54.

13 Michael O'Pray, *Avant-Garde Film: Forms, Themes, Passions* (London: Wallflower, 2003), p. 43.

14 Roger Horrocks, *Len Lye: A Biography* (Auckland: University of Auckland Press, 2002), p. 135.

15 Horrocks, *Len Lye*, pp. 36–7. Elizabeth Sussex, *The Rise and Fall of the British Documentary: The Story of the Film Movement Founded by John Grierson* (Berkeley, CA: University of California Press, 1975), p. 84.

16 Simon Brown, 'Dufaycolor: The Spectacle of Reality and British National Cinema', AHRC Centre for British Television and Film Studies, 2005, www.bftv.ac.uk/projects/dufaycolor.htm#_ftn48 [accessed 11/02/2011]; and Horrocks, *Len Lye*, pp. 36–7.

17 Ian Christie, 'Colour, Music, Dance, Motion: Len Lye in England: 1927–44', in *Len Lye*, eds Roger Horrocks and Jean-Michel Bonhours (Paris: Centre Georges Pompidou, 2000), p. 188. See also Luke Smythe's 'Music and Image in Len Lye's

Direct Films', *Journal of New Zealand Art History*, 27 (2006), pp. 1–14.

18 Sigmund Freud, 'A Note upon the "Mystic Writing Pad" (1925)', in *Standard Edition of the Complete Psychological Works of Sigmund Freud*, vol. 19, eds and trans. James Strachey and Anna Freud (London: Hogarth Press, 1971), p. 234.

19 Kevin Jackson, 'The Joy of Drooling: In Praise of Len Lye', in *The Projection of Britain: A History of the GPO Film Unit*, eds Scott Anthony and James G. Mansell (London: BFI/Palgrave, 2011), p. 95.

20 Logan Esdale, 'Gertrude Stein, Laura Riding and the Space of Letters', *Journal of Modern Literature*, 29.4 (2006), p. 103.

21 Lye, 'Getting Out of the Griffith Technique [1967]', *Figures of Motion*, p. 54.

22 Horrocks, *Len Lye: A Biography*, p. 166.

23 Horrocks, *Len Lye: A Biography*, p. 225.

24 P. Adams Sitney, *Eyes Upside Down: Visionary Filmmakers and the Heritage of Emerson* (Oxford: Oxford University Press, 2009), p. 283.

2
Somewhere in the city

> Somewhere in the city of New York there are four or five still-unknown objects that belong together. Once together they'll make a work of art. (Charles Simic, 'Where Chance Meets Necessity')[1]

A typical decade in the life of New York City can be as eventful as several anywhere else, and the 1950s was no exception: as other Americans cruised the freeways of post-war contentment, New Yorkers appeared restless, and out of kilter with the national *Zeitgeist*. Their city, unlike Pittsburgh, Cleveland, or Detroit, had never been a crucible of mass-production methods. Instead, its landscape and demography had facilitated small and medium-scale manufacturing, and a large, localised harbour economy. Although at the centre of world finance and international diplomacy, child poverty in the city increased steadily throughout the decade, and daily life in its tenements was blighted more by gangs, guns, and dilapidated public housing than 'Communism, Korea, and Corruption', to borrow one of Eisenhower's electoral slogans from this era. Nothing if not consistent in its contrariness, however, organised labour in the city remained politically influential, and resistance to urban renewal schemes grew, as Jane Jacobs and civic activism attempted to interrupt the hegemony of Robert Moses and automotive fascism. In the Village, and on the Lower East Side, a flourishing culture of experimentalism in the arts was also contradicting the 'Age of Conformity', preparing the ground – and 'underground' – for the radicalism of the 1960s.

Just as surrealism, and the wider modernist project, had left its mark on London's documentary film culture in the 1920s and 1930s, so too New York's filmmakers of the 1950s and

1960s were attracted to the methods of the city's avant-garde artists. While various technological as well as social factors facilitated the popularity of New York street photography and documentary film after the Second World War, there was also a new motivation to develop aesthetically distinctive practices in both fields: if documentary film and photography were to be more than instruments of journalistic discourse, ephemeral purveyors of news for an ever-expanding mass media, or – worse still – merely personal exercises in visual communication, they had to create expressive forms that challenged commonplace assumptions about the objective nature of their own image systems. In this regard, the experimental techniques being championed by the New York School proved fortuitous, especially given the importance of actual, everyday, *documented* urban experience to the emerging artists, poets, composers, and critics associated with the School.

Joseph Cornell's films from the 1950s oscillate between documentary and abstract art, realism and symbolism, between everyday life in a material city, and a more metaphysical phenomenon where birds, children, trees, parks, and passers-by can acquire an allegorical or numinous aspect: 'Cornell brings the neutrality of a newsreel cameraman to his shots ... he lingers on the most ordinary things [and] the ordinariness melts into the silveriness of the images, takes on a mysterious dimension.'[2] His dozen or so short films made during the 1950s, document both real worlds and dream worlds. As with his boxes, collages, and earlier film work, nostalgia is a key sentiment: these cinematic wanderings around New York, and into its spaces, are also journeys into a past, orphic quests to retrieve and reconstitute a lost world from found reality, from remnants of the present.

City/documentary

After the Second World War, the US government continued to relax immigration quotas, ending the isolationism that had prevailed throughout the 1930s, and – more controversially – early 1940s. Migrants once again flowed into New York,

and neighbourhoods in Queens and Brooklyn became home
to a new generation of post-war refugees, who soon registered
the presence of their deracinated sensibility. The influence
of Europe, and especially the debates within and around neo-
realism, featured in the city's fledgling independent film culture, especially in its rejection of conventional documentary
representations of reality, a reality that now seemed, more
than ever, to be an ambiguous and deceptive phenomenon.[3]
The realisation that the field of the film image had been per-
manently transformed by recent history coincided with the
emergence of a new avant-garde attitude, an attitude that also
countered assumptions about documentary filmmaking (as a
transparent and socially instrumental activity) by exploring a
much looser, and abstract approach. When Amos and Marcia
Vogel established the Cinema 16 *cinémathèque* in 1947, for
example, they were not only influenced by figures like Maya
Deren (who was successfully producing independent films,
and creating audiences for her work) but also by the possibility
of working with people involved in collaborative experiments
with other artists and writers, and who shared a broad commitment to improvisatory and associative filmmaking techniques.[4]
In another part of New York's avant-garde culture, the Living
Theatre project – also founded in 1947 – was developing a radical praxis between audience and performance that was not just
breaking down the so-called 'fourth wall' but was explicitly
foregrounding the particularity of each theatre experience, and
encouraging a politics of participation in which experimental
theatre could be a catalyst for social engagement, and drama
itself, a mode of documentary practice.[5]

As well as this redefinition of documentary realism, the
1950s also coincided with a golden age of New York street
photography, and – following in the footsteps of photographer-
filmmakers like Paul Strand and Willard Van Dyke – many
photographers took advantage of recent innovations in film
technology to translate their photographic method into the
language of documentary film, Weegee's (Arthur Fellig) 1948
short, *Weegee's New York* (b&w, 20 min.) being a seminal case
in point.[6] Post-war New York street photography was an espe-

cially reactive and dynamic form; often with minimal attention paid to the formalities of framing and composition, its
photographs did not so much evince the absence of precision
as insinuate the presence of cinema. Helen Levitt, for instance,
collaborated with fellow photographer Janice Loeb, and James
Agee, in a film that chronicled everyday working-class life in
East Harlem, *In the Street* (1948/1952, b&w, 14 min.). Parts of
the film used the same 'sneak camera' technique Levitt and
Loeb had deployed in their photographic work, and the thematic orientations of Levitt's early work (informed by her
experiences as an art teacher in rundown public schools, and
earlier involvement with Loeb and Agee working on Sidney
Meyers' *The Quiet One* (1948, b&w, 64 min.)) is reflected in the
film's emphasis on capturing natural images of children, especially children playing on the streets, throwing flour-bombs,
and dressing up as adults. Free from script and voice-over
narration, *In the Street* emerges as a sensitive, unsentimental
depiction of impoverished, overcrowded urban life, a world at
odds with a more glamorous Manhattan.[7] As Manny Farber
commented in his contemporary review of the film: 'The great
American outdoors, once a wide-open prairie for adventures is
here, in one shrunken pocket of New York City, a place of possible terror to people who spend their time looking at it with
100 per cent distrust.'[8]

A preoccupation with the lives of poor, marginalised ten-
ement children characterised much New York photography
and film during the late 1940s and early 1950s, especially educational and social documentaries, such as *The Quiet One*, or
Angry Boy (Alexander Hammid, 1950, b&w, 31 min.).[9] Other
New York films featuring children tended to combine documentary realism with a fictionalised narrative; *Little Fugitive*
(Ray Ashley, Morris Engel, and Ruth Orkin, 1953, b&w, 80
min.) – with its own 'sneak camera' depictions of Brooklyn
and Coney Island – was both influenced by neo-realism,
and became itself an influence on contemporary European
cinema (for example, *The Red Balloon/Le Ballon rouge* (Albert
Lamorisse, 1956, col., 35 min.), and *400 Blows/Les quarter cents
coups* (François Truffaut, 1959, b&w, 99 min.)). Like Levitt

and Loeb, Hammid, Orkin, and Engel were also professional photographers. On the other hand, Robert Frank and
Alfred Leslie's celebrated collaboration with Jack Kerouac
and friends, *Pull My Daisy* (1958, b&w, 30 min.), tends more
towards madcap theatricality than visual or cinematographic
originality – although, there are continuities of mood and temperament between its manic *mise en scène* and the darkly ironic
textures of the photography in Frank's influential book, *The
Americans* (1958). William Klein's *Broadway by Light* (1959,
Argos, 12 min.), meanwhile, is an abstract colour film, a montage of neon that reputedly provoked Orson Welles to declare
it 'the first film I've seen in which colour is absolutely necessary'. Although, it is reasonable to compare the vivid images in
Broadway by Light with the distinctive black-and-white photographs that comprise much of Klein's first book, *Life is Good
& Good for You in New York: Trance Witness Revels* (1955), the
film is in fact closer to Klein's abstract and typographic art,
and the experimental films made by other contemporary New
York visual artists in the 1950s (as opposed to the documentary
photographers), for example: *N.Y., N.Y.* (Francis Thompson,
1957, col., 15 min.); *Highway* (Hilary Harris, 1958, b&w, 5
min.); and Shirley Clarke's *Bridges-Go-Round* (1958, col., 4
min.) and *Skyscraper* (1959, col., 20 min.).

Like Klein, Rudy Burckhardt was also a painter and photographer before he began making films, in a long career
that involved working with various artistic forms and communities. More in the style of Walker Evans than Weegee or
Klein, Burckhardt's New York photography resisted rough-
hewn expressionism, and the transformation of familiar locations into bizarre underworlds; even a cursory comparison of
Burckhardt's New York photographs from the late 1930s with
some of Klein's from the 1950s and 1960s, for example, reveals
markedly different styles of photographing similar places.[10]
Originally from Basle, Switzerland, Burckhardt arrived in
New York from Europe in 1935, with his companion, Edwin
Denby, the internationally acclaimed (and recently retired)
US dancer who was now turning his talents to travelling, and
writing poetry and criticism.[11] Although Denby introduced

Burckhardt to the New York School, and the Bohemia of 7
Middagh Street, the Living Theatre, and the eventful cafés and
bookstores of the Village and the Lower East Side, he soon
found his own niche, and began photographing and filming the
shapes, shades, and facades of the city. While there are similarities between his visual style and Precisionism, Burckhardt's
method of representing architectural scale and urban space was
perhaps influenced more by the de Stijl group, something that
may well have caught the eye of Cornell (when looking for
a photographer whose formal austerity would complement –
rather than compete with – his own techniques).[12] Like Cornell,
poetry often figured in Burckhardt's visual art, especially the
poets of the New York School, and his films conversed regularly with work from the 1950s and 1960s by John Ashbery,
James Schuyler, Kenneth Koch, Barbara Guest, and Frank
O'Hara. As well as making films either explicitly inspired by
their poetry, or including poems read by the poets themselves,
he also photographed artists – such as Jackson Pollock, Joan
Mitchell, and Willem and Elaine de Kooning – for galleries
and magazines, and worked closely with composers like Aaron
Copland, Virgil Thompson, and Paul Bowles. Interestingly, the
stylistic qualities associated with the New York School and its
circle (vernacularity, 'nowness', satire, excess, etc.) are typically
tempered in Burckhardt's photography and filmmaking from
this period by a more restrained aesthetic, as in, for example:
Up and Down the Waterfront (1946, 8 min.); *The Climate of New
York* (1948, 21 min.); *The Automotive Story* (1954, 15 min.); and
Eastside Summer (1959, col., 12 min.).

Burckhardt's method configures the geometry of the city,
abstracting buildings, streets, pavements, signs, figures and
crowds into discernible lines, crosses, and contrasts. By foregrounding oblique perspectives and sharply angular shadows,
his framing typically accentuates the scale and verticality of
New York, a technique he perfected in the 1940s (e.g. in photographs such as 'Flatiron Building in Summer, *c*.1947', 'Herald
Square, 1947', or 'Times Building, *c*.1948'). In his homage to
the Brooklyn Bridge, *Under the Brooklyn Bridge* (1953, b&w,
15 min.), for example, he applied this approach to a cinematic

rendering of a landmark mythologised (in a precisionist idiom) by artists such as Charles Sheeler, Joseph Stella, and Georgia O'Keefe; and its iconic allure had already proved irresistible to any number of notable photographers (from Alfred Stiegliz to Berenice Abbott), poets (especially, Hart Crane's *The Bridge* (1930)), novelists (e.g. John Dos Passos's dystopic vision in *Manhattan Transfer* (1925)), and Hollywood (perhaps, most frequently in the 1950s, or Frank Sinatra serenading its grandeur in *It Happened in Brooklyn* (Richard Whorf, MGM, 1947). Burckhardt's film comprises five parts, each representing different aspects of everyday life beneath, beside, and just beyond the bridge. The first part of the film, for example, begins with a montage of hand-held shots of the gothic-style exterior of the Eagle Warehouse, the camera lingering on its robust windows, elaborate arches, exterior signs and architectural ornaments, and its intricately patterned brickwork, before the film cuts to shots of modern Manhattan office blocks, with their exactness, blankness, and geometric simplicity. This sequence culminates in a long shot of the bridge, taken from a point between two large buildings: reframing Brooklyn Bridge – as both monument and metaphor – is the central theme of the film. The Eagle Warehouse, for example, was originally home to the *Brooklyn Eagle*, the newspaper edited by Walt Whitman in the 1840s. Although written before the bridge was constructed, Whitman's penultimate poem from *Leaves of Grass* (1855), 'Crossing Brooklyn Ferry', haunts Burckhardt's film, invoking both the influence of Whitman's democratic aspirations – his poetry's availability to everyday, everyman experience – on the New York poets (especially, Ashbery), as well as Sheeler and Strand's *Manhatta* (1921, 10 min.). Other sequences from the film depict the demolition of a large building (using some time-lapse photography), labourers and other workers eating in a busy café, boys swimming in the East River, and women leaving work, before the film ends with a series of panoramic shots of the bridge, set against the Manhattan skyline. For Burckhardt, the bridge does not just physically link Manhattan to Brooklyn, it delineates its own community, who live, work, eat, and play under its hospitable shadow.

3   *Under the Brooklyn Bridge*

This vision of the bridge is also evident in a photographic
diptych he produced the following year, 'View from Brooklyn:
Parts I and II' (1954). This is another instructive example of
Burckhardt's compositional technique, and his preference for
nuance over flamboyance. In 'View from Brooklyn: Part I', he
uses a wide-angle lens to photograph a section of his Brooklyn
Heights apartment, including a chair, desk, radiator, waste-
paper basket, some postcards on the wall, and the window,
with its view of an old ferry pier on the East River, and the
Manhattan skyline beyond.[13] In the second photograph, 'View
from Brooklyn: Part II', everything in the apartment appears
identical to 'Part I' except the view from the window, which
now frames the bridge in all its iconic splendour, with just
a small part of the pier now visible. Essentially, this diptych
reveals how even a slight – initially indiscernible – shift in perspective, can produce a markedly different image. Admittedly,
one of the postcards has now disappeared, and another has
been moved, etc. but the true subject of Burckhardt's diptych

is photography itself, and the essentially ambiguous, indeterminate nature of perspective.

In the mid 1950s, Burckhardt collaborated with Cornell,
and together they completed ten short films. By this time,
Cornell was adopting an approach to filmmaking that dif-
fered somewhat from his earlier methods. Instead of editing
together found footage from old feature films, and adding
tints, musical accompaniment (soundtracks), and trickery (as
in *Rose Hobart* (1936, 17 min.)), or adopting even more complex compilation-collage techniques (as in the 1940 trilogy
of short silent films, subsequently completed and restored by
Larry Jordan (*Cotillion* (8 min.), *The Midnight Party* (3 min.),
and *The Children's Party* (8 min.)), he had become interested
in a more tentative documentary method. Instead of splicing
magical voyages from found footage of fairytale books, puppet
shows, circus acts, celestial bodies and exotic places, etc., he
now wanted to incorporate places and times from reality, to
record the familiar, making films from original documentary
footage of New York rather than found footage from elsewhere.
Editing was still important and Cornell maintained a clear
directorial sense of the images and sequences he wanted from
his 'cameramen' (i.e. Burckhardt, Stan Brakhage, and Jordan).
In a 1993 interview Burckhardt reminisced about working
with Cornell:

> I remember he telephoned me one morning. I hadn't really
> met him and his work, his boxes, had been shown at the Stable
> Gallery, and the Egan Gallery … and he said, 'Do you want
> to make a film with me?' and I said, 'yes'. We made a date to
> meet at Union Square on a cold Saturday morning in December.
> I brought the camera and he brought some rolls of film, and
> I brought the tripod. He said he didn't like to use that – it's
> too technical. So from then on everything was handheld. A few
> times it was real magic, all kinds of things. I noticed all kinds of
> things that I hadn't looked at before. For example, that statue
> that's there. I never looked at it before.[14]

New York/Nyack

Joseph Cornell was born into a relatively prosperous family on Christmas Eve, 1903, in Nyack, a Hudson River village once renowned for its master yacht builders, and as the birthplace of Edward Hopper (in 1882). After the death of Cornell's father in 1917, the family struggled financially and had to move away from Nyack, eventually settling into a rented timber-frame home on Utopia Parkway, in Flushing, Queens. On leaving boarding school, Cornell lived the rest of his life in this house, caring for his disabled younger brother, and their elderly mother. Although he found irregular work as a designer and fabric salesman, and struck up friendships and correspondences – especially, with other artists, and a few curators – essentially, he was a shy and reclusive figure whose inarticulate, sublimated sexuality was never far from the surface of his imagination. Cornell idealised European culture, especially Romantic painters and composers, and canonical French literary figures such as Jean-Jacques Rousseau, Gérard de Nerval (*Aurélia*), Stéphane Mallarmé, Marcel Proust, and Antoine de Saint-Exupéry – although he rarely travelled, and never beyond the East Coast. A practising Christian Scientist, who – much to the chagrin of his Methodist mother – liked quoting from the writings of Mary Baker Eddy to visitors, Cornell was also influenced by the Transcendentalist tradition in US letters; Whitman, Emily Dickinson, and Henry David Thoreau were especially important writers for him. Given his receptiveness to such a variety of influences, ranging from Romanticism and transcendentalism to symbolism and surrealism, it is perhaps easier to categorise Cornell's art in terms of what it is *not*, rather than what it *is* – and it is not realism.[15]

Many of his boxes, for example, are love letters to images and ghosts, to former or living female stars of the cinema (Hedy Lamarr, Lauren Bacall, Gloria Swanson, Greta Garbo), unattainable ballerinas, female sopranos, and other performers out of the past. In box-constructions such as *Taglioni's Jewel Casket* (1940), or *Homage to the Romantic Ballet* (1942), for instance, Cornell placed glass imitation ice cubes on velvet lining, or a blue glass shelf, inside a wooden box. An inscription on the inside of the lid briefly relates a story from the life of the famed ballerina, Marie Taglioni (1804–84). One night, while travelling through Russia, her coach was stopped by highwaymen. Before leaving the scene of their robbery, the leader of the gang placed a panther skin rug on the snow and requested that Taglioni dance for him – which she did, in the silent, midwinter moonlight. Thereafter, she always kept a glass ice cube in her jewellery box during performances, as a lucky *momento*. Throughout the 1940s, the contemporary ballerina Tamara Toumanova was also the subject of various Cornell boxes, collages, and 'snow bowls'. He was particularly fond of *Swan Lake* – and Tchaikovsky's music – and images of Toumanova sometimes feature in his work in her role as Odette, 'Princess of the Swans': for example, the collage print, *Homage to Tamara Toumanova* (1940), or one of his most well-known box-constructions, *A Swan Lake for Tamara Toumanova: Homage to Romantic Ballet* (1946).

Cornell's boxes, miniature cabinets, bric-a-brac assemblages, and collages involve the containment of objects – and images as objects – picked up, gleaned from flea markets and dime stores, and meticulously archived into folders and dossiers until there was enough for a new work. Many of the objects and images related to birds, seashells, maps, glass (and imitation glass) ornaments, and postcards (generally, from hotels). The boxes are framing structures, dioramas, *petits théâtres* that enclose fragments of stories, narrative possibilities, images, the flotsam and jetsam of desire. Never merely a collagist of the quotidian, the apparent surrealism of this art jolts conventional notions of proportion (and appropriation), craft (and consumption), artefact (and artwork), and not only crosses the boundaries between collage, sculpture, and installation art, but also between modernism and folk art; the inspiration for his boxes, for example, doubtless owes something to North American vernacular arts and crafts (for example, 'whimsy bottles' and nautical ornaments) associated with upstate towns and villages along the Hudson, towns like Nyack.

Cornell began collecting old film reels and discarded studio stock in the early 1930s, around the same time his work began to be exhibited at Julien Levy's recently established gallery of modernist art on Madison Avenue. His relationship with Levy and Duchamp has tended to give an exaggerated impression of his closeness to Surrealism, while undervaluing his more enduring – if less intellectually fashionable – attachment to Symbolism, and Transcendentalism. Despite an initial enthusiasm for Surrealism, and a willingness to see his work exhibited alongside that of Duchamp, Max Ernst, and Dalí, Cornell recoiled at some of the movement's depictions of sex and sexualised forms, its endorsement of doodling and automatic writing, and he was never likely to surrender the 'white magic' of dream and fairytale to the dark rationalism of Freudian interpretation.[16] Levy included some of Cornell's collages in the gallery's Surrealism exhibition in January 1932, and gave him a solo exhibition later that year, which included some shadow boxes, and collages incorporating small mechanical toys, and other 'found' objects (*Jouets surréalists* and *Glass Bells*). In 1936, Cornell made his first film (*Rose Hobart*) by re-editing an original print of a humdrum 'jungle' melodrama, *East of Borneo* (George Melford, 1931, Universal) into a blue-tinted, eighteen-minute compilation of sequences (projected at 16 pfs), featuring the actress, Rose Hobart. By way of a musical accompaniment to each screening, Cornell liked to play tracks from a Nestor Amaral album, *Holiday in Brazil* – Amaral and his Cuban salsa-style band ('The Continentals') had supported another of his favourite stars during the 1940s, Carmen Miranda. Discarding the film's narrative scaffold and its original soundtrack, Cornell constructed what is essentially a documentary of desires, a fantasy of *East of Borneo*, or, as Jonas Mekas put it: 'The Hollywood unreality is transported into Cornellian unreality.'[17] When *Rose Hobart* was first screened at Levy's gallery in 1939, a jealous Salvador Dalí stood up, kicked the projector, and denounced Cornell as a pickpocket of other people's dreams.

Throughout the late 1930s and early 1940s, Cornell continued to make compilation-collage films – by editing sequences from old Hollywood motion picture reels, and various industrial and travelogue documentaries. In the style of the 'Children's Trilogy', some of these works drew extensively from puppet and fantasy films (e.g., *Jack's Dream* (*c*.1938, 4 min.)), while others depicted travels to faraway places, and constellations – voyages into the firmament by fragments of film, photography, and pages from books (e.g. *Bookstalls* (*c*.1940, 11 min.), and *New York–Rome–Barcelona–Brussels* (*c*.1938, 10 min.), or *By Night With Torch and Spear* (*c*.1942, 8 min.)). Although he rarely screened his work in public, in 1949 he did accept an invitation from Robert Motherwell to hold a couple of film evenings at Subjects of the Artist, an 'art school' Motherwell had recently co-founded with Mark Rothko, David Hare, and William Baziotes. (These events, and others like them, were never easy or entirely successful for Cornell.) An avid cinema-goer, Cornell also wrote a film script about a hapless photographer (*Monsieur Phot (Seen Through a Stereoscope* (1933)), and over the years he assembled a large collection of rare film reels, film-related books and magazines, photographs, and memorabilia.[18] Female stars – like the famed ballerinas – also became subjects for Cornell's artwork – 'a hallmark of his artistic production' – and many of his well-known boxes and collages are portrait-homages to stars such as Lauren Bacall and Jennifer Jones: 'A pleasure to watch, but impossible ever to reach, the dematerialized light-filled expanse of the moviestar image offers spaces of voyage and fantasy and is thus the perfect subject for the artist's perambulating portraiture.'[19] Cornell's homage pieces to women and child stars, ballerinas, and mythical figures also have a sepulchral aspect, just as his boxes are sometimes reminiscent of columbarium walls, or cemeteries, like the one on Montjuïc, in Barcelona. In such art, as in the story of Marie Taglioni's winter *momento*, or the writings of Mallarmé and Proust, there is the inviolable intimacy between desire and death.

Impressed by Burckhardt's lucid, precise photographic style, Cornell had known him for several years, and first suggested they collaborate on a film in the early 1950s. At that time, Cornell was also contributing cover designs and occasional pieces to Lincoln Kirstein's *Dance Index*, a journal that also regularly featured the writing of Denby.[20] Moreover, the New York School poets, whose methods of assemblage and association, and enthusiasm for European – especially, French and surrealist – literature and art found a convivial resonance in Cornell's art: Frank O'Hara's 1955 'box' poem, 'Joseph Cornell', and John Ashbery's 'Pantoum: Homage to Saint-Simon, Ravel, and Joseph Cornell' (originally published in his first collection, *Some Trees* (1956)), inaugurated a significant genre of literary conversations with the artist's work that continues to this day.[21] The most successfully achieved films from Cornell's collaborations with Burckhardt are: *The Aviary* (1955, b&w, silent, 11 min.); *Nymphlight* (1957, col. Silent, 7 min.); *A Fable for Fountains* (1957, b&w, 6 min.); *Angel* (1957, col., silent, 3 min.); and *Seraphina's Garden* (1958, b&w, silent, 8 min.), a film also reminiscent of the opening sequence of shots from Marie Menken's *Glimpse of the Garden* (1957, col., 5 min.). As in the case of Cornell's other collaborations, a number of these films exist in different cuts, with alternative titles and soundtracks (or none at all). For example, footage from the original version of *The Aviary* reappears as *Joanne, Union Square* (1955, b&w, silent, 7 min.), and sequences from *A Fable for Fountains* became *Mulberry Street* (1956, b&w, silent, 9 min.), and *Children* (1957, b&w, silent, 8 min.); both of which exclude any shots of Suzanne Miller (an actress Cornell had befriended), who features in *A Fable for Fountains: Fragments*. Burckhardt also re-edited *The Aviary*, cutting the sequences that featured Jean Jagger (Cornell's niece), and making the film shorter (by nearly six minutes). Burckhardt also offered Cornell an alternative cut of *A Fable for Fountains/Mulberry Street*, retitled *What Mozart Saw on Mulberry Street* (1957, b&w, 6 min.). Generally, however, Cornell had little interest in other people's versions of these films. Reflecting on Cornell's reaction to *What Mozart Saw on Mulberry Street*, for example, Burckhardt later commented: 'He just didn't like any kind of manipulation … he wanted there to be things that accidentally came his way … he left most everything in the films.'[22]

These films differ formally from the earlier compilation-collage works, and Cornell's preoccupations in the 1950s had less to do with found footage filmmaking than using the film camera to archive, or capture in a sequence, a particular place, time, and mood in the life of the city. Films such as *The Aviary*, *Nymphlight*, *Angel*, and *A Fable for Fountains* are not necessarily observational or diaristic precursors to Andy Warhol's early films, or the so-called 'lyrical' works of the New York Underground. If anything, Cornell's filmmaking in the 1950s merely affirms his rejection of realism, and his attachment to a symbolic perception of the world, and a belief in the existence of an alternative reality, a reality made visible through accidents, coincidences, and mundane mysteries. Cornell's disagreement with Burckhardt's editing suggestions is more theological than formal, and is related to an underlying ambition to reconcile his art with the teachings of Christian Science, and the pursuit of a 'spiritualization of vision'.[23]

The Aviary was filmed in Union Square Park. Since the early 1930s, Cornell had been making his aviary boxes, a practice inspired by both a fascination with Victorian glass cases filled with stuffed birds, and his habit of observing caged birds in pet shop windows, and imagining the exotic homelands of these creatures: parakeets, canaries, cockatoos. The aviary boxes usually contain a cut-out image of a bird, and various objects, especially pictures and postcards – souvenirs from their imaginary travels. There is also a mystical aspect to Cornell's birds: for example, the religious symbolism of doves, and their similarity to angels. *The Aviary* evokes these associations, as well as Oscar Wilde's fairytale, 'The Happy Prince'. The centrepiece of its *mise en scène*, for example, is the park's monumental fountain, donated in the 1880s by a local philanthropist 'to promote the virtue of charity' in the city. Drinking water is dispensed through the mouths of four ornamental lion heads protruding from each of the fountain's sides. The fountain also serves as a plinth for a large statue of a woman carrying an infant in one hand, and holding an older child with her other hand. In the film, birds are framed perched on this statue, and – briefly – on an imposing equestrian statue of George Washington. The statues, trees, pathways, and human visitors are viewed through branches and hedges, and occasional oblique angles,

4 *The Aviary*

creating a 'bird's-eye' perspective: birds flock and flit around the trees; a young woman strolls up to the fountain and examines its decorative engravings before walking away; an elderly man feeds some of the birds; a group of boys discard their bicycles, jump over a fence and start wrestling on the grass; a male dwarf strolls across the park, assiduously smoking his cigarette. The sequences involving Jean Jagger were encouraged rather than staged by Cornell, and while he was specific in his instructions to Burckhardt – what he wanted the camera to frame, and how – Cornell's goal was not solely to represent Union Square Park in a picturesque or nostalgic light but to reveal it as a world simultaneously here and elsewhere.

Nymphlight also enunciates a coexistence of material and metaphysical realities. Like *The Aviary*, the film transforms a very public space into a sacred grove, or clearing, where alternative truths are invited into existence. The film opens with shots of a teenage girl (Gwenn Thomas)[24] running along the wall of the New York Public Library, skipping into Bryant Park, wearing a Victorian-style evening dress, and carrying a white shabby antique parasol. It is a sunny day, and she charms the park with her carefree, swirling élan, or nymphlight. A gardener is caught in long shot, tending one of the park lawns, as the camera adopts the girl's point of view, observing birds flying around under the park's loose canopy of trees, before they congregate around the base of a fountain. The film then cuts to the street, and frames the Horn and Hardart Automat restaurant on 42nd Street. This was, perhaps, one of Cornell's favoured Manhattan eateries, and its rows of token slots and glass-fronted meal compartments may have inspired some of his own shadow boxes and slot machines; in the 1940s and 1950s, the franchise was also synonymous with the sponsorship of NBC's *Children's Hour*. Maintaining this observational style, the film then returns to the park, to New Yorkers milling around, sitting on benches and reading newspapers, before cutting to another medium–long shot: a different girl, wandering aimlessly along one of the pathways, a documentary *Doppelgänger* of the theatrical Gwen Thomas figure. This sequence is followed by several seemingly random observational shots: a woman walking her dog, and other people passing through the park; all of whom are entirely oblivious to the filmmakers, or entirely indifferent to them. The camera then lingers on a large fountain, closing in on the water, as if to emphasise the identity of Gwenn Thomas's character as a local naiad, or water-sprite – a logical association given Cornell's fascination with the Ondine myth, and its relationship to the nineteenth-century ballerina, Fanny Cerrito, whose performance in Jules Perrot's original *Ondine, ou La Naïade* (1843) became the stuff of legend. Throughout his career, Cornell made various Ondine-related artworks, for example: 'Portrait of Ondine' (1940), 'Fanny Cerrito in *Ondine*' (1947), and 'Ondine's Owl' (1954), which he made as a gift to Audrey Hepburn (who was starring that year at the 46th Street Theatre in a revival of Jean Giraudoux's stage version of *Ondine*). In *Nymphlight*, the Ondine-figure is the invention that enables Cornell to represent Bryant Park according to *his* sense of the real, and not according to some realist fantasy of unmediated transparency: for Cornell, the park exists as both dream-world and real-

5   *Nymphlight*

world, and the film attempts to document that phenomenon: '*Nymphlight* is a tribute to Bryant Park, a space, like the interiors of Cornell's boxes, both liminal and enchanted where children play like sprites, where the park's past remains alive in the present'.[25] Cornell had intended a musical soundtrack for the film, made up entirely of Debussy's 'Cloches à travers les feuilles/ Bells Through the Trees [lit. *leaves*]', from the composer's 1907 series, *Images*. Instead, he subsequently made a four-minute version of *Nymphlight*, cut the shots featuring Gwen Thomas, and titled it: *Cloches à travers les feuilles* – effectively reversing the technique he had used in his re-editing or reassembling of *East of Borneo* into *Rose Hobart*.

   A Fable for Fountains: Fragments adopts a similarly versatile, polyvalent documentary form, and was further re-edited by Cornell and Larry Jordan in 1965 as *A Legend for Fountains*.[26] The film takes its title from the epigraph to a Federico García Lorca poem, 'Your Childhood in Menton'/'Tu Infancia en Menton' ('Yes, your childhood: now a fable of fountains'), which is then repeated in the opening and closing lines of

the poem. 'Your Childhood in Menton' was first published in
Poet in New York/Poeta en Nueva York, the collection of poems
Lorca wrote in 1929–30, during his stay in the city; and he took
this epigraph for 'Your Childhood in Menton' from a poem by
one of his friends and mentors, Jorge Guillén's 'Gardens'/'Los
Jardines'. Both poems invoke innocent excess in the face of
adult sorrow, and their metaphorical range more closely resembles a symbolist poetics than a surrealist one. In this regard,
Cornell's own outlook and artistic temperament was particu-
larly compatible with that of Guillén, and the Lorca of *Poet in
New York*. Throughout the 1950s, the work of both poets was
being translated and discussed by people like Denby, Charles
Henri Ford, Langston Hughes, Rolfe Humphries, Kerouac,
and the New York School (O'Hara's 1957 poem, 'Failures of
Spring', for example, or Allen Ginsberg's collection, *Howl
and Other Poems* (1956), which is indebted to Lorca's 'Ode to
Walt Whitman'). English-language (and bilingual) editions of
Lorca's *Selected Poems*, his *Three Tragedies*, and Ben Belitt's
translation of *Poet in New York* were all published in New York
in 1955. Guillén had emigrated to the US after the Civil War
in Spain, and throughout the 1940s and 1950s, he taught at
Wellesley College, continued to publish poetry and criticism,
was awarded a Guggenheim Fellowship in 1954, an American
Academy of Arts and Letters Award of Merit Medal (Poetry)
in 1955, and in 1956 he was invited to deliver the prestigious
Norton Lectures at Harvard. In the 1930s, the Spanish Civil
War had been a catalyst for political debate among New York
intellectuals, and in the 1950s its spectre was readily invoked
in the face of McCarthyism – of which Rose Hobart, herself,
fell foul. The rediscovery of Lorca's poetry (and persona) in
the mid 1950s, like the presence of Guillén, was related to
that contemporary history. It was also an acknowledgement of
the city's increasingly vibrant Hispanic culture, as were other
contemporary developments (for example, the founding of the
Queen Sofía Spanish Institute in 1954), events (major exhibitions at MoMA dedicated to the work of figures such as Antoni
Gaudí (1957–58) and Joan Miró (1959)), and possibilities (an
evening in November, 1959 when Miles Davis and Gil Evans

began work recording *Sketches of Spain*, at the CBS 30th Street Studio).[27]

Cornell's film opens with a low-angle tracking shot of a young woman (Miller) descending an apartment block staircase. Just as Lorca repeats the epigraph to 'Your Childhood in Menton' in the poem's opening line, so too Cornell repeats this opening sequence in his film. Lorca's New York poems are characterised by nostalgia for childhood, identified by the poet as a place of freedom from painful adult emotions, the brutality of modernity, and a city in the throes of unprecedented economic chaos. In Lorca's collection, fraught streets and overwhelming skyscrapers mingle with dream images, and become correlatives to the poet's own sense of emotional disintegration. As the young woman in Cornell's film leaves the apartment building, shots of her walking through a darkened passageway, and boys peering (perhaps, at her) through a door-window demonstrate Burckhardt's talent for framing the liminal. The film alternates images of – and references to – childhood and adulthood, birds and buildings, movement and stasis, and its use of inter-titles from 'Your Childhood in Menton' (e.g. '... tokens and traces of chance') does not so much structure the film and organise its fragments, as sustain its conversation with the poem. Likewise, images of writing (for example, graffiti, hand-written and printed signs), and various shop front windows in Little Italy displaying dolls, toys, religious statues (a 'Child of Prague'), and mannequins, are moments when the imaginations of Cornell and Lorca coincide, when another 'shrunken pocket of New York City' is transformed into a metropolis of symbols.

In November 1957, Cornell took Burckhardt to film at Flushing Cemetery, a fifteen-minute walk from his home on Utopia Parkway. On this occasion, he wanted to make a film to commemorate the recent death of Pavel Tchelitchew, the Russian émigré artist he had first met in the 1940s, through Kirstein and his circle. Tchelitchew was Charles Henri Ford's lover, and their promotion of surrealism and Dada (especially, in the pages of Ford's and Parker Tyler's magazine, *View*) countered the seemingly relentless popularity of the abstract

expressionist movement at that time. Cornell was especially
fond of Tchelitchew, who had also designed the set and costumes for Giraudoux's 1939 original Paris production of the
stage version of *Ondine*. The completed film, *Angel*, comprises
eighteen hand-held shots, and lasts just over three minutes.
The camera position is stationary in all the shots, except one
eighteen-second panning shot, which is also the longest in
the film. *Angel* is silent, and – like *Nymphlight* – it was shot on
Kodachrome colour. There are two recurrent features in the
film: a monumental statue of an angel; and a large water font
surrounded by rhododendrons and daisies. Two consecutive
shots of the statue open and close the film, and a further two
appear in the middle, suggesting that Cornell may have had a
triptych (or ode) structure in mind for *Angel*. The statue shots
are taken from different perspectives, at noticeably different
times of the day; as tree branches sway in the breeze, and
clouds move across the sky, the angel remains permanent and
immoveable, its sensually sculpted bodily form enjoined to
the uncanny enormity of its wings. The shots of the font or
pond, the sunlight reflected in the water, and the surrounding flowers, are rendered by Burckhardt in differing scales
and textures, registering the presence of a breeze, gentle rain,
changing light, as Sitney asserts: 'The film is a masterpiece of
tonal nuance'.[28] A number of these shots frame the reflections
of trees in the water, or leaves floating on, or just below, its
surface. The film's homage to Tchelitchew is evident not only
in its images of change and metaphors of mortality, but also
in how it juxtaposes these reflexive, immaterial forms with
the solidity of the monument. More particularly, *Angel* pays
homage to how Tchelitchew's paintings fuse anatomical and
religious imagery, body and soul. For Cornell, death is merely
a passing from one existence to another, and the reality of that
other existence is visible in the world around us, in memories
of Nyack, and his attraction to the otherworldliness of children, birds, ballerinas, and also angels. The closing shot in
Angel calls to mind Jorge Luis Borges's 1929 essay: 'A History
of Angels':

I always imagine [angels] at nightfall, in the dusk of a slum or a vacant lot, in that long, quiet moment when things are gradually left alone, with their backs to the sunset, and when colours are like memories or premonitions of other colours. We must not be too prodigal with our angels; they are the last divinities we harbour, and they might fly away.[29]

Cornell/Brakhage

When it was finally announced that the Third Avenue elevated train line (the El) was to be demolished in May 1955, Cornell decided to make a film (originally, entitled *The Last Days of the El*) to commemorate the passing of this – the last remaining – elevated train service in Manhattan. Before 'commissioning' Stan Brakhage as his cameraman, Cornell had approached Burckhardt, who seems to have been enthusiastic about the idea but was frustrated by the public transport authority's decision only to grant him permission to photograph 'on the portions ordinarily used by passengers'. Later in 1953, Burckhardt wrote to Cornell, informing him he had 'given up the idea of the El movie', and was now working on a documentary with Koch, O'Hara, and Jane Freilicher, *The Automotive Story*.[30] The El was an important remnant of an older New York, and as its demolition became imminent, photographers and filmmakers sought to capture it – and its world – before the bulldozers moved in. In D. A. Pennebaker's first meaningful foray into documentary filmmaking, *Day Break Express* (1953, col. 5 min.), for example, Duke Ellington's eponymous soundtrack complements a cinematographic style influenced by the El paintings of Ashcan artist John Sloan (whose 'Pigeons' (1910) must surely have appealed to Cornell). The heyday of New York's Elevated train system coincided with the emergence of the Ashcan School of Art, and the system's rail stock and stations feature in numerous paintings and pencil-drawings by another of its leading lights, Edward Hopper. Another film, Carson 'Kit' Davidson's *3rd Ave El* (1954, col. 11 min.) – which was nominated for an Academy Award ('Best Short Subject: One Reel') – offers a witty take on the El, using a harpsichord rendition of Haydn's

Concerto in D to accompany its jaunty array of camera angles, montage structures, and special effects. Although *3rd Ave El* is structured around a series of vignettes involving passengers (a photographer, a drunk man, a young girl, and a pair of lovers) – who attempt to dislodge a dime jammed between two slats in the flooring – the film successfully renders different points of view from the train, at different times of the day and night. Like Brakhage, Davidson's eye was intuitively drawn to the shadow and silhouette formations created by the El network's latticework of steel beams and cross-frames, its ornate railings and turnstiles, and coloured-glass surrounds.

Brakhage has just arrived in New York from San Francisco, where he had attended the California Institute of Fine Arts. Although still in his early twenties, he was already an experienced filmmaker, and he had begun to experiment with various abstract techniques, as in, for example, his *Unglassed Windows Cast a Terrible Reflection* (US, 1953, b&w, 29 min.). Orbiting within and around Maya Deren's Village circle, he collaborated briefly with John Cage, and Edgard Varèse (who had an important influence on his future artistic development), and he was introduced to Cornell by Tyler Parker. Once recruited by Cornell, Brakhage received some train tickets and a roll of Kodachrome in the post from him. In return, Brakhage made *Wonder Ring* (1955, col., 5 min.), a short kaleidoscopic montage of some of the El's shapes, movements, and vistas. After the flickering, handwritten, opening title sequence, the shots are repeatedly structured and double-framed by doors, windows, ceilings, railings, bridges, junctions, and corner buildings. Brakhage uses these random architectural frames to create a series of affecting juxtapositions. Making *Wonder Ring* was an important exercise for Brakhage. It was not his first attempt at a more abstract style of filming, but its content and visual texture registers the growing influence of Deren, as well as that of the wider New York avant-garde. For Cornell, however, *Wonder Ring*, was – if anything – much too abstract and *structural*: Brakhage's subject matter seemed to be motion and light, and not the actual, felt experience of travelling on the El. There is some controversy around what happened next but it seems that Cornell collected the outtakes from Brakhage's film, flipped (or flopped) them, spliced them together, and reversed the lettering of the film's title, thereby creating a new film, *Gnir Rednow* (1968, col., 5 min.).[31] In so doing, Cornell created more than simply inbound and outbound versions of the one film; he wanted this new work to be projected forward and backward in a continuous loop, preserving more completely that shuttering, swaying sensation familiar to El passengers: 'For Cornell, the Third Avenue El is not just a structure, it is a structure of feeling'.[32] Although comprising Brakhage's discarded images of/from the El and its environs, Cornell's film also fixes more readily on the El's *framings*, on where and what the passengers see: to travel on the El was an experience akin to going to the cinema, or looking at any number of 'Cornell boxes'.

Despite the *Wonder Ring* incident, Cornell remained friendly with Brakhage, and later that year invited him to collaborate on *Centuries of June* (1955, 11 min.); although this time, Cornell minimised the potential for any misunderstandings by working directly with his 'cameraman', a practice he would also follow when filming with Burckhardt. As with *Gnir Rednow*, *Centuries of June* attempts to capture on film both an actual architectural structure on the verge of demolition, and the mysterious sensation of a time and place evoked by that structure. In this case, the condemned building was a mid-nineteenth century timber 'Tower House' along Utopia Parkway, a building that perhaps reminded Cornell of his own former family home in Nyack, as well as fairytales, such as the Grimm's 'Rapunzel'. *Centuries of June* exemplifies Cornell's sense of filmmaking as an artistic means of subordinating history to nostalgia, facts to the phenomena that produce them – rather than just an instrument of documentary representation or record. As with *A Fable for Fountains*, he again chose a title from a poem – in this case, one of Emily Dickinson's ruminations on life after death, and the condition of eternity:

There is a Zone whose even Years
No Solstice interrupt –
Whose Sun constructs perpetual Noon
Whose perfect Seasons wait –

Whose Summer set in Summer, till
The Centuries of June
And Centuries of August cease
And Consciousness – is Noon. (1865)[33]

Just as Dickinson's poem comprises two quatrains that cohere
around an alternative rhyme pattern, Cornell's film can also
loosely be divided into two parts – the first, rendering the
house in terms of neglect, death, and a possible supernatural
presence, while the second associates it with children, playfulness, and happiness. In the first part – or quatrain – of the film,
trees and overgrown bushes, shrubbery, and grass are shown
surrounding the house, and a large outhouse or stable is adja-
cent to the main building. The camera diffidently tracks along
the eaves and the exterior timber panelling – some of which is
darkened by damp and rot – before the film cuts back to the
tower, and again, moves – probes – across the side wall, before
pulling into a full shot of the front porch, and the impressive
exterior staircase that leads into the house. The porch is also
flanked on either side by overgrown trees, grass, and bushes –
all of which threaten to envelope it completely. The tentative
hand-held framing also gives the impression the house is not
so much derelict as haunted, and its ghostly, gothic aura is
accentuated by the fleeting appearance of a figure (an elderly-
looking man using a stick – probably, Cornell, himself), who
emerges from behind a side wall. The sense of the macabre is
also conveyed by the presence of an unusual forked tree in the
main yard, and smoke emanating from a small, mysterious
fire behind it. Brakhage also took two (Derenesque) p.o.v.
shots from inside the house, one from the top of the tower,
and another through a misty upstairs window. The film then
suddenly cuts to a medium close-up of a boy sitting nonchalantly in the grass, outside the house. This is followed by a
longer shot of a group of girls returning home from school
along the parkway, before the camera tracks a particular boy
and girl, as they pass the house. An already demolished property next door has now become a ready-made playground for
children in the area, and Cornell concludes the film by giving

those children – and play – the last word: buildings may come and go, fall into neglect and disrepair, but – true to his own peculiar amalgam of a Romantic, Rousseauist, and Christian Scientist idealisation of childhood – eternity, for Cornell, is associated with eternal childhood, a return to 'centuries of June'.

Transfiguring documentary fragments of New York into fables and allegories is at the crux of Cornell's artistic method, demonstrating the similarities between his films and his other artworks, especially the box constructions, which also transform ordinary, everyday, found *documents* into artistic works that cohere around a complex set of cultural and metaphysical associations. It is in this sense that Cornell's films from the 1950s ought to be situated more securely within the context of the photography, painting, and poetry associated with the New York School, and – therefore – that longer, wider debate on the relationship between modernist expression and documentary representation.

Notes

1   Charles Simic, 'Where Chance Meets Necessity', *Dime-Store Alchemy: The Art of Joseph Cornell* (New York: NYRB, 1992), p. 14.

2   Jed Perl, *New Art City: Manhattan at Mid-Century* (New York: Vintage, 2007), p. 297.

3   The US reception of *Rome, Open City/Roma città aperta* (Rossellini, 1945, 103 min.) in 1946, for example, is a good case in point, and contemporary reviews by Bosley Crowther (*New York Times*), John Mason Brown (*Saturday Review of Literature*), and James Agee (*The Nation*) are included as an appendix to a collection of essays on the film – Manny Farber's review (*The New Republic*) is also worth reading, although it is not republished in that appendix. Sidney Gottlieb, ed., *Roberto Rossellini's Rome Open City* (Cambridge: Cambridge University Press, 2004), pp. 161–70; and Robert Polito, ed., *Farber on Film: The Complete Film Writing of Manny Farber* (New York: Library of America, 2009), pp. 278–9.

4   Amos Vogel, *Film as a Subversive Art*, 2nd edn (New York: C. T. Editions, 2005); Scott MacDonald, *A Critical Cinema: Interviews*

with Independent Film-Makers, vol. 3 (Berkeley, CA: University of California Press, 1998), pp. 13–40.

5 Judith Malina and Julian Beck, *Paradise Now: Collective Creation of Living Theatre* (New York: Vintage, 1972).

6 Incidentally, the soundtrack for *Weegee's New York* is Leonard Bernstein's score for Jerome Robbins's 1944 ballet, *Fancy Free*, which also features on the soundtrack of *Rear Window* (Alfred Hitchcock, 1958).

7 Roy Arden, 'Useless Reportage: Notes on Helen Levitt's *In the Street*', *Afterall*, 6 (autumn/winter 2002): www.afterall.org/jour nal/issue.6/useless.reportage.notes.helen.levitts.street   [accessed 12/08/2013].

8 Manny Farber, *Negative Space: Manny Farber on the Movies*, new edn (New York: Da Capo, 1998), p. 46. Farber's praise for Levitt's skills as an editor may have persuaded Lionel Rogosin to employ her (albeit briefly and unhappily) on the post-production of *On the Bowery* (1956). See also Jack C. Ellis, 'American Documentary in the 1950s', in *Transforming the Screen: 1950–1959*, ed. Peter Lev (Berkeley, CA: University of California Press, 2003), pp. 257–77.

9 Hammid worked with Irving Jacoby on *The Quiet One*, and both were involved in Willard van Dyke's 1948 documentary, *The Photographer* (b&w, 26 min.), Hammid as editor, and Jacoby as writer.

10 For example, Burckhardt's 'Checkerboard Tiled Wall Detail with Ice Cream Advertisement' (1938) and '"Eagle" Barber Shop Window' (1939), and Klein's 'Candy Store' (1955) and 'Antonia Simone Barbershop' (1961).

11 On his return to New York, for example, Denby was commissioned by Orson Welles and John Houseman to adapt a WPA Federal Theatre production of Eugéne Labiche's *Un Chapeau de Paille d'Italie/Horse Eats Hat* (1851), at the Maxine Elliott Theatre, with an original score composed by Bowles. See also Catherine Gunther Kodat's 'Reviewing Cold War Culture with Edwin Denby', in *American Literature and Culture in an Age of Cold War*, eds Steven Belletto and Daniel Grausman (Iowa City: University of Iowa Press, 2012), pp. 37–58.

12 Andrea Henderson and Vincent Katz, *Picturing New York: The Art of Yvonne Jacquette and Rudy Burckhardt* (New York: Bunker Hill, 2008), pp. 75–7.

13 According to the poet Ron Pagett, this apartment still belonged to Jane Bowles – who had returned to New York at that time to

work on the production of her play, *In the Summer House*, at the Living Theatre. 'Poetry Lectures: Oral History Initiative: On Frank O'Hara: Informal Conversation between John Ashbery and Ron Pagett'. Podcast: www.poetryfoundation.org/features/audioitem/3418 [accessed 11/06/2013].

14 Martica Sawin, 'Oral History Interview with Rudy Burckhardt' (14 January 1993), *Archives of American Art, Smithsonian Institution*, www.aaa.si.edu/collections/interviews/oral-history-interview-ru dy-burckhardt-12098 [accessed 13/06/2013]. See also Rudy Burckhardt and Simon Pettet, *Talking Pictures: The Photography of Rudy Burckhardt* (Cambridge, MA: Zoland, 1994), p. 128.

15 See Lindsay Blair's *Joseph Cornell's Vision of Spiritual Order* (Edinburgh: Reaktion, 1998), pp. 76–84.

16 For example, in a letter to Alfred Barr, dated 13 November, 1936, Cornell stated: 'I do not share in the dream theories of the Surrealists. While fervently admiring much of their work, I have never been an official Surrealist, and I do believe that Surrealism has far healthier possibilities than have been developed' (Archives of MoMA, qtd. in Blair, *Joseph Cornell's Vision of Spiritual Order*, pp. 209–10, n. 13).

17 Jonas Mekas, 'The Invisible Cathedrals of Joseph Cornell', in *A Joseph Cornell Album*, ed. Dore Ashton (New York: Da Capo, 1974), p. 164.

18 See Annette Michelson's important article on this phase of Cornell career: '*Rose Hobart* and *Monsieur Phot*: Early Films from Utopia Parkway', *Artforum*, 11.10 (June 1973), pp. 47–57; P. Adams Sitney, 'The Cinematic Gaze of Joseph Cornell', in *Joseph Cornell*, ed. Kynaston McShine (New York: MoMA, 1980), pp. 70–2.

19 Jodi Hauptman, *Joseph Cornell: Stargazing in the Cinema* (New Haven, CT: Yale University Press, 1999), p. 5.

20 Lincoln Kirstein, 'On Edwin Denby', *New York Review of Books*, 30.14 (29 September 1983), pp. 4–5.

21 See also Jonathan Safran Foer, ed., *Convergence of Birds: Original Fiction and Poetry inspired by Joseph Cornell* (London: Penguin, 2001).

22 Qtd. in Deborah Soloman, *Utopia Parkway: The Life and Work of Joseph Cornell* (Boston, MA: Boston MFA), 1997, p. 243.

23 Doss, Erika, 'Joseph Cornell and Christian Science', in *Joseph Cornell: Opening the Box*, Jason Edwards and Stephanie Taylor eds (Berlin: Peter Lang, 2007), p. 132.

24 Nowadays an art photographer in her own right, Gwenn Thomas is the daughter of Yvonne Thomas, the artist and close friend of Burckhardt and Denby.

25 Haupman, *Joseph Cornell: Stargazing in the Cinema*, p. 199.

26 According to P. Adams Sitney, this revised title was in keeping with another translation of Lorca's poem by Edwin Honig, from the *Selected Poems* (1955), which was considered superior to the Belitt version. See Sitney's 'Cinematic Gaze of Joseph Cornell', p. 83.

27 See John Szwed, *So What: The Life of Miles Davis* (New York: Simon & Schuster, 2002), pp. 208–9.

28 Sitney, 'Cinematic Gaze of Joseph Cornell', p. 87.

29 Jorge Luis Borges, 'A History of Angels [1929]', in *Jorge Luis Borges: Selected Non-Fiction*, ed. Eliot Weinberger (New York: Penguin, 1999), p. 19.

30 Burckhardt, letters to Cornell: dated 6 May 1953 and 8 August, 1953. Joseph Cornell Papers: General Correspondence, box 1, folder 48. *Smithsonian Archives of American Art*: www.aaa.si.edu/collections/joseph-cornell-papers-5790 [accessed 25/04/2013].

31 'My study of the prints made it absolutely clear that the films shared not one single *shot between them*' (Mark Toscano, 'Archiving Brakhage', *Journal of Film Preservation*, 72 (2006), p. 23).

32 Sunny Salter, 'Farewell to the El: Nostalgic Urban Visuality on the Third Avenue Elevated Train', *American Quarterly*, 58.3 (2006), p. 873.

33 'There Is a Zone Whose Even Years [1020]', in *The Poems of Emily Dickinson: Reading Edition*, ed. R. W. Franklin (Cambridge, MA: Harvard University Press, 1999), p. 421.

3

Questioning the frame

I reel off a small lovely rustling revolution
and I fall and I murmur and I sing. (Lucebert)[1]

In autumn 1957, Allen Ginsberg and Peter Orlovsky found
themselves in Amsterdam, looking hither and thither for their
friend and fellow Beat writer, Gregory Corso. The obscenity
trial that had followed the publication of *Howl and Other Poems*
(1956) had left Ginsberg tired, and pessimistic about the US. He
had decided to travel, and after visiting Paul and Jane Bowles
at their home in Tangier, he and Orlovsky headed to Paris,
where they had earlier made arrangements to stay with Corso
– who, in the meantime, had flitted to Amsterdam. Although
the three poets soon returned to Paris – and subsequently
stayed there until the early 1960s (at the now famous 'Beat
Hotel') – the Dutch capital had proved a revelation to them:
it was inexpensive, convivial to their lifestyle, and the place
where they discovered solidarity with other anti-establishment
poets, such as Simon Vinkenoog and Adriaan Morrën.[2] The
city had, after all, quickly returned to the avant-garde fray after
the war, and by the mid 1950s it had witnessed the formation
of various small but influential groups such as REFLEX, the
Fiftiers (De Vijftigers), the Experimental Group Holland (De
Experimentele Groep Holland), and CoBrA.[3] This vibrant culture of modernism would also leave a lasting impression on a
young Dutch photographer, filmmaker, writer, and jazz enthu-
siast: Johan van der Keuken.

Encouraged by his grandfather, Van der Keuken took up
photography when he was 12, and was already exhibiting and
publishing work before he left Amsterdam in 1955, to study at

the Institut des hautes études cinématographiques (IDHEC). In Paris at that time, figures such as Joris Ivens, Herman van der Horst, Bert Haanstra, and even the up-and-coming Louis van Gasteren, were enjoying international acclaim as documentary filmmakers, and Van der Keuken's chances of making a name for himself among such luminaries must have seemed slim.[4] As if his chosen artistic field was not crowded enough, there was also the formidable hinterland of post-war French cinema to contend with – not least, the emerging brilliance of the New Wave – as well as the achievements of French photojournalism, a cultural project that had already involved Ed van der Elsken, another Dutch photographer-filmmaker, surrealist, and important presence in Van der Keuken's life and work. This was a milieu as rich in talent as it was rife with the usual coteries and rivalries, and while he had to work hard to make a name for himself, other developments closer to home fed his ambitions.

Despite his criticisms of the modern history and politics of the Netherlands, Van der Keuken never abandoned Amsterdam, and in terms of situating his work within a contemporary Dutch film culture, he consistently showed himself to be adept at producing work that was *both* socially engaged and formally experimental.[5] While his sympathies were socialist, as is apparent in his films from the 1960s through to the mid 1980s, he disliked any form of political and social behaviour that struck him as dogmatic, or intellectually obtuse.[6] While the classic Dutch documentary schools, and the emergent *cinéma vérité* tradition in France, taught him much about film and photographic technique, he also learned a great deal about the language of images and structures of audiovisual perception from the same poets, painters, and musicians who befriended Ginsberg and his companions. Throughout his career, for example, Van der Keuken maintained an attachment to the philosophy and legacy of CoBrA, with its rejection of André Breton and Parisian surrealism in favour of a more primitive, *simplistic* approach to paint, texture, and poetry. Although its official lifespan was short (1948–52), CoBrA attracted a number of artists who were personally and professionally close to Van der Keuken, and who collaborated with him at various times, namely: Lucebert (poetry and painting); Remco Campert and Bert Schierbeek (poetry); Van der Elsken (film and photography); and Willem Breuker (music). As this reference to Breuker and Van der Elsken suggests, jazz – especially, free jazz – shaped Van der Keuken's artistic development. His *Big Ben/Ben Webster in Europe* (1967, b&w, 31 min.), for example, was one of his own favourite films, and he (with his wife, the filmmaker and sound editor, Noshka van der Lely) often created soundtracks comprising a distinctive admixture of contemporary and classical jazz compositions. In this respect, CoBrA's post-war assault on both official and pseudo-oppositional versions of reality encouraged him to experiment with new and unorthodox perspectives on the politics of poverty, injustice, and violence.

Image/frame

Although Van der Keuken had studied cinema at IDHEC, he had initially concentrated on photography before becoming interested in how the basic formal properties of film – movement, time, and 'abolishing the standstill' – countered the expressive limitations of the photograph.[7] It was intimacy, indecisiveness, impermanence, and spontaneity that were to become the hallmark of his cinematic style, rather than some of the more fashionable photographic tendencies of the day: objectivity, 'decisiveness', stability, and fastidiousness. Not surprisingly, the question of the frame, and how this question defines Van der Keuken's visual style, is a recurrent topic in literature on his work. According to Serge Daney, for example, image-making for Van der Keuken involves a constant tension between the discursivity of the filmic fragment and its irreducibility, between the camera-eye that frames the image, and the frame as pure phenomenon, 'un trop de cadre' that threatens to overwhelm – 'partout, toujours' – the possibility of double-framing, reframing, or deframing.[8] Bérénice Reynaud has also commented on how Van der Keuken's approach to framing 'is not only motivated by a creative doubt about the nature of "the Real", but also by an implicit questioning of his own mental processes, of the role he plays in the construction/distribution of "knowledge"'.[9] Meanwhile, in an essay chiefly concerned with Van der Keuken's photography, Alain Bergala has described his style of framing as being 'torn between [a] taste for sustaining images … and the feeling that the act of cutting off part of reality and giving it meaning against its own will embodies a harmful arrogance'.[10] In the case of documentary film, this aesthetic of 'reticence' liberates the image from predetermined illustrative or storytelling functions, allowing greater scope for unexpected, genuinely artistic possibilities.

Van der Keuken's framing techniques, his experiments in frontal, free-form cinematography, and associative colour and sound configurations, give expression to a core uncertainty – or ambivalence – about the authority of the documentary image, and the reality of representation. His films will often juxtapose sequences that disrupt a narrative trajectory with sudden discontinuities, distractions, and detours – some improvised, others staged. Dramatic contrasts of colour and sound, in particular, can unsettle a seemingly realistic, documentary depiction and disturb the natural flatness of the image, accentuating movement, plasticity, and instability. François Albera – another influential critic of Van der Keuken's work – has commented on how his filmmaking deliberately keeps in play two potentially contradictory impulses: on the one hand 'there is reality, the world, profuse, multiple, impossible to embrace in its entirety, but which must be seen, ceaselessly filmed and recorded'; and on the other, 'there is the fact that every image and every sound in this world, captured by the operator's machines will find themselves, one way or another, projected into another order of reality, that of representation rounded down to one or two dimensions'.[11] Even when his filmmaking appears to hold a discernible ideological or moral stance, the formal strategies he adopts – the oblique framing, expressionistic shot structures, elliptical montage, abstract soundtracks, etc. – are drawn from an aesthetic that readily acknowledges the unreliable indexicality of the image, and the essential vulnerability of its narrative formations.

Not surprisingly, Van der Keuken's filmmaking and photography is at its most successful when it is a curious, spontaneous – sometimes, disorientated – participant in the essential strangeness of both the foreign and the familiar, new landscapes and cities, experiences, and people. Like Chris Marker, he admired Robert Musil's unfinished trilogy of novels, *The Man Without Qualities/Der Mann ohne Eigenschaften* (1930–42), citing on one occasion – tellingly – a remark in the novel that 'we are motivated both by a strong desire to meet and make contact, and at the same time by an absolute horror of meeting someone else'.[12] Locating places where art and documentary converge enabled Van der Keuken to keep in play a tension between the act of filming and fact of being filmed, the camera as both witness and agent, both recording device and expressive resource.

Silence

A Moment's Silence/Even stilte (1963, col., 10 min.) offers an early example of Van der Keuken's characteristic approach to configuring coexisting times and places that relate to one another not only in a suggestive, implicit, or reticent form but in a way that can suddenly – scandalously, even – reveal a lie at the heart of collective – especially national – memory. Much less photographic and lyrical than his first city film, *Paris at Dawn/Paris à l'Aube* (1960, b&w, 10 min.), *A Moment's Silence* juxtaposes its Amsterdam sequences to unravel some of the mythology surrounding Dutch resistance during the war, and the politics of its commemoration.

With the Nazi bombardment of Rotterdam on 14 May 1940, Queen Wilhelmina and her family, along with some members of the Dutch government, fled to London. A Reich administrator was immediately installed with powers to rule by decree. As in France, Belgium, and elsewhere, the local civil service machine and most of the political elite remained *in situ* and found acquiescence preferable to resistance. By the end of 1940, the Dutch Nazi Party (NSB) had over 80,000 members (and over 100,000 by the autumn of 1943), and at least 25,000

Dutch civilians volunteered to fight in the Heer and Waffen-SS during the occupation period. Jews were soon segregated, and easily identified thanks to the bureaucratic efficiency of the Dutch civil service; and NSB members frequently – openly – assaulted them in the street. Closed Nazi guilds were established, political parties were abolished, and conscientious local censors acted promptly to ban music by Jewish composers, and performances by Jewish musicians. Fritz Hippler's *The Eternal Jew/Der ewige Jude* (1940) was screened regularly in every major Dutch town. In May, 1942 there were 140,000 Jewish people living in the Netherlands; by the time of the Nazi withdrawal in June, 1944, 105,000 had perished in or on their way to the Death Camps. There were of course Dutch citizens who resisted the policies of the Nazis – especially those who participated in the communist-led 'February Strike of 1942', and others (Van der Keuken's older brother, for example) who joined the Resistance at home and abroad – but active and passive collaboration was commonplace until 1944, and the mistreatment of returning Jews after the war remains a source of considerable embarrassment, if not shame, in the Netherlands.[13]

A Moment's Silence opens with a (stock) high-angle, long shot of Amsterdam coming to a silent standstill for two minutes to commemorate the dead of the Second World War, during National Memorial Day, on 4 May. Van der Keuken's opening shots centre on trams, a train, cars, cyclists – on transport, traffic, movement – before cutting to two crowds gathering on either side of Dam Square. The film then cuts to a shot from another part of the city in which schoolchildren are being lead across a road by a clergyman (or some such teacher/authority figure), and then to shots of other children laughing and carrying flowers, before returning to the square: silent, respectful, motionless. There then follows a shot of a young girl carrying a box across a bridge; a military-style lorry is visible in the background, and then a woman is shown playing with her dog. And so the film continues, developing into a seemingly random tableau of a day in the life of Amsterdam: men salvaging iron on the canal, children playing among the rubble of a building site, and so forth. The soundtrack comprises background noise, snatches of music and dialogue, and the film contains a number of jump cuts and shots partially obscured or fragmented by branches of trees, or parts of buildings. In another sequence, the camera lingers on a man lighting a small fire on a riverbank, followed by a shot of heavy rain splashing on water, and washing over the pavement. A funfair is next and children screaming with excitement, frantically waving their orange flags (presumably, this footage is from the annual *Koninginnedag* or Queen's Day celebrations). The children are filmed running away from one of the carnival clowns. The carnival motif is carried into the subsequent shots of a parade with marchers in national costume, uniforms, military bands, police on motorbikes, soldiers, and crowds cheering. Finally, the film returns to its initial 'moment's silence', the national commemoration where the crowd is now shown dispersing, and returning to their everyday lives (or 'Etc'. as the end title puts it).

At one level, *A Moment's Silence* is a loose chronicle of urban life, another experimental 'city documentary', a period piece paying homage to works such as Joris Ivens's *Rain/Regen* (1929, b&w, 12 min.), as well as the collage techniques associated with CoBrA. On another – more metaphorical – level, it is a cinematic rumination on recent Dutch history and what an officially sanctioned 'moment of silence' is really attempting to silence. Between the opening and closing shots of the official commemoration, all the images collected and included refer obliquely to the war and occupation, and to a child's-eye view of these experiences: Van der Keuken was a two-year-old when the Nazis assumed control of the Netherlands, and he was nearly six when the war ended. These images, taken from three years' worth of actuality filming, build up to a crescendo of marching uniforms, a circus clown, and cheering crowds before cutting to a lone teenage boy throwing baskets in the morning mist. In this sense, the film is also a companion piece to *Velocity 40–70/De snelheid 40–70* (1970, col., 25 min.), which commemorated the thirtieth anniversary of the occupation by accompanying a filmed interview with an Auschwitz survivor

with shots and footage of contemporary Holland, and images
gleaned not from (found) newsreel archives and photographs
from that historical period but rather from the silence Van der
Keuken *observes* in 1970.

Art

Lucebert (pseudonym of Lubertias Jacobus Swaanswijk,
b. 1924) was an important figure within Dutch avant-garde
circles throughout the post-war period, and an exact contemporary of Van der Elsken. His working-class father and
grandmother reared him within a strict Calvinist tradition
(his parents divorced when he was two), and in 1944 the
Occupation government sent him to a Forced Labour Camp
in western Germany. As a poet and artist, Lucebert co-founded
the Experimental Group Holland, and the Fifties, and aligned
himself to CoBrA, which mainly comprised artists from
Copenhagen, Brussels, and Amsterdam (hence its name). As
a poet, Lucebert was influenced by various automatic, oneiric
and nonsense techniques derived from Dada and surrealism.
He was also attracted to what were viewed at the time as radical
political causes. In addition to contemporary social issues in the
Netherlands, his poetry refers to post-colonial Indonesia (the
Dutch East Indies), the history of slavery, Salvador Allende,
and other figures such as the prominent South African anti-
apartheid activist and poet-painter, Breyten Breytenbach. In
particular, Lucebert shared with other Fifties writers a sceptical attitude towards the humanist value system endorsed by
their parents' generation, a scepticism borne of contempt for
what those values had permitted (and, in some cases, encouraged) during, and after, the Second World War. Lucebert's
angry, anarchic cast of mind was well suited to CoBrA, with its
own rejection of bourgeois hypocrisy, and the tyranny of sensibility. Artistically, CoBrA insisted on a return to the primitive,
the ludic, the fantastic and folkloric, to the art of children, and
the doodling of adults. Inaugurated in 1948, the movement
was generally left-wing in its sympathies, and within a year,
it comprised over fifty members, and encompassed the work

of artists such as Karel Appel, Aldo van Eyck, Carl-Henning Pederson, Constant Nieuwenhuys, and Asger Jorn (who would prove instrumental in finding a home from home for CoBrA in the Situationist International). In its endorsement of spontaneity, hedonism, and 'the creaturely', CoBrA encouraged an unbridled expressionism that sought to shock and scandalise the otherwise austere, disappointed demeanour of European culture in the aftermath of the war.[14]

Van der Keuken's *Lucebert: Time and Farewell/Lucebert: Tijd en afscheid* is a trilogy comprising short films from 1962, 1964, and 1994. The 1962 film was produced for the Ministry of Culture as part of a series on contemporary Dutch artists; the other films in that series examined the lives and work of two Dutch cartoonists (Yrrah (Harry Lambertink), and Opland (Rob Wout)), and Shinkichi Tajiri, the Dutch-American sculptor, painter and filmmaker (and CoBrA member). These artists – at least in the 1950s and 1960s – shared Lucebert's sceptical, anti-authoritarian outlook. The first part of the Lucebert trilogy uses a recording of Lucebert reading some of his poems to accompany the images, complementing and counterpointing the gestural and formal affinities between writing and ink-drawing, a *graphic* interrelationship that fascinated the CoBrA artists. The 1962 film also includes inserts of numerous still photographs of Lucebert, as well as more intimate images, such as footage of him with his children at a birthday party, all of which tends to accentuate an important contrast between the playfulness of the man, and the seriousness of the world outside: 'We are sleepwalkers in a cold circus', his voice intones at one point. The film makes a clear association between the grotesque, monstrous images and masks that Lucebert draws and paints as an adult, and his childhood (and experiences during the war).

The second part of the trilogy is more sophisticated in terms of its structure, and production values (and was shot in colour). Again, the hardships of Lucebert's childhood are the *leitmotif* and the film opens with a montage of archive images of Amsterdam slums in the 1930s, and press cuttings and other photographs of rioting and police brutality at this time. Van der Keuken establishes a set of juxtapositions: a grainy, black-and-white portrait photograph of Lucebert as a child, followed by a close-up of his contemporary artwork (dark, dense oil paintings of monstrous faces and distorted bodies, with shark-like teeth and bulbous eyes), and a montage of images from the riots, followed by shots of deserted street scenes from this part of the city in the mid 1960s. In addition to Beuker's music, the soundtrack includes animal – or 'creaturely' – noises and other strange wheezing and breathing sounds. Van der Keuken uses rapid montage techniques to 'exhibit' the paintings gathered together in Lucebert's studio before cutting into an extended sequence of the artist at work, in front of his canvas, painting a homage to bullfighting, and Picasso (one of his heroes). Towards the end of this part of the film, the colour red becomes dominant, bleeding into a montage of raw meat and a row of pigs' heads lined up at a butcher's stall (with cacti, crabs, and so forth) before cutting back to the more wholesome amusements of family life. This sequence is then followed by shots of a calf getting its throat cut open, before being bled to death (in itself, anticipating similar images from Van der Keuken's later *The Way South/De weg naar het zuiden* (1981, 145 min.). Lines from Lucebert's ironic anti-racism poem, 'A Big Gruff Negro' conclude the film.

Although the final part of the trilogy is a more personal homage – made to mark Lucebert's death (in 1994) – it is also a reflection on death and grief, more generally. The images of his art and writing are still present but Lucebert's absence is now the subject of the film, and so too, therefore, Van der Keuken's own melancholic attitude after that death. The camera pans and surveys the empty apartment and immaculate studio. It seems to virtually caress the scribbles and bric-a-brac of Lucebert's daily distractions, returning from time to time to a shot of a rocking horse in the room that one would expect to be stationary but which, instead, rocks involuntarily – *mysteriously*. At one point, the camera makes a sudden charge at a page of writing on Lucebert's bed (deathbed), as if trying to consume its own image, to banish the absence, touch another reality. The paintings appear again and – like dominoes – involuntarily fall back and collapse in a neatly edited sequence. The next shot shows children in the studio, playing and laughing. Again, their freedom and innocence seems in contrast to Lucebert's paintings of dark, cold, surreal ogres. The film closes with another shot of that grainy portrait photograph of the artist as a child: 'Everything of value is defenceless.'[15]

History

During the Siege of Sarajevo (April 1992–March 1996), Van der Keuken was invited to the inaugural Sarajevo Film Festival – 'Beyond the End of the World: 23 October – 3 November, 1993' – where he screened two of his most recent films: *Face Value* (1991, 120 min.), and *Brass Unbound* (with Rob Boonzajer Flaes, 1993, 106 min.). Haris Pašović, who had attracted international attention when he produced Susan Sontag's controversial Sarajevo production of *Waiting for Godot* earlier that year, co-organised the festival, and he appears in the opening sequences of *Sarajevo Film Festival Film*, accompanying his Dutch guests – Van der Keuken, and his producer/sound engineer, Frank Vallenga – across the dangerous city. Ordinary Sarajevians are filmed moving hurriedly through the streets, ferrying water and provisions, amid the noise of sporadic sniper fire, and trundling UN personnel carriers. Occasionally, Pašović talks to the camera about the Festival, the war, and surviving in this city. The second part of the film features Marijela Marjeta, a young student of architecture who lives in an apartment block at the frontline with her sister, and their blind, elderly father. Throughout the Festival, she regularly attends screenings and Van der Keuken's short film pays tribute to the unassuming heroism of such people, and the importance of the cinema to their sense of hope and citizenship, as well as offering them a temporary escape from the war outside.

From its pre-title sequence, shot from the dark, rattling interior (*camera obscura*) of a moving Land Rover (where Van der Keuken's bouncing hand-held camera captures images of the streets outside through the vehicle's 'letter-box' windscreen)[16] to the final close-up of Marijela Marjeta's face in the cinema,

Sarajevo Film Festival Film repeatedly returns to images of actual and figurative frames, screens, light and darkness, emphasising the contrast between the harsh, dangerous circumstances of life in and around the apartment blocks and the relative shelter of the cinema space. Shots of the bullet-holed and bomb-damaged buildings, the ever-precarious water supply, and the family's difficult life in their cramped, darkened apartment are intercut with images of the cinema projector lights, the appreciative Festival audience, and grainy sequences from films being screened: cinema in spite of chaos. Towards the end of *Sarajevo Film Festival Film*, Van der Keuken films the two sisters together outside their apartment block, preparing a small garden for vegetables. In the background, incessant but still distant sniper fire is heard; the women keep low and calmly continue their work, forming an 'improbable *tableau vivant*, derived from Jean-François Millet's *The Angelus/L'Angelus* (1859)', as Bergala observes (though his *The Gleaners/Des glaneuses* (1857) is the more likely influence).[17] Suddenly, the shots become loud and immediate. Van der Keuken drops his camera. It continues to film as it turns into the ground before he manages to catch it, and frame his shot. The sisters now crouch on their knees but seem stoical, as Marijela tries to ease the tension: 'I suppose it's not dangerous', she remarks, nervously. Then, a sniper returns fire from a high apartment block directly above them, and Van der Keuken instinctively directs his camera into the vicinity of the gunfire as the danger passes. The film cuts to its closing shot of Marjeta's face, engrossed in a screening at the Festival, while her voice-over recounts what the war has taken from her. This final image also calls to mind François Truffaut's reputed statement to the critic, Gene Siskel, that there is nothing more beautiful in the cinema that seeing the light from the screen reflected on the upturned faces of the audience.

Despite its hand-held informality and immediacy, *Sarajevo Film Festival Film* succeeds because its fragmentariness is merely narrative: cinematically, it is a remarkably coherent vignette of a day in the life of a city under siege. In nearly every shot in the film, there are windows, or doorways of some sort, size, or description: a ghostly mannequin in a display cabinet, a discarded threshold, large black sheets on a clothes line, rows of derelict cars pock-marked with bullet holes and rust, and even as the camera randomly scans the film festival audience, the framing is careful, and available to fortuitous associations. The success of the Festival as an event is a testament to the endurance of the city and this – for Van der Keuken – symbolises something deeply civilised amid the terrorism of the Serb mortars and machine guns, and the trundling impotence of the UNPROFOR. At that moment, caught in the crossfire, when the rolling camera falls from his hands amid violence and fear, in the spilt second when circumstances seem to frame the filmmaker and not vice-versa, when reality supplants *vérité*, *Sarajevo Film Festival Film* becomes a different kind of documentary: 'There, miraculously, just for once, [Van der Keuken] received an immense, enigmatic recompense for all his pains: he really did touch reality.'[18]

In 'touching reality', the film also seemed strangely prophetic of an event that would forever associate the Netherlands with the war in Bosnia: the Srebrenica Massacre. In July 1995, Ratko Mladić's Serbian troops occupied the designated 'safe enclave' of Srebrenica and Zepa, and proceeded to expel its Bosniak (Muslim) population of inhabitants and refugees, systematically murdering the males (estimates put their death toll in excess of 8,000), and raping and torturing the women and girls. The victims had been promised protection in this so-called 'safe haven' by the United Nations. In reality, the UNPROFOR units in question not only failed to prevent the genocide but their negligence, and naive attempts to negotiate a deal with the Serbs, unwittingly facilitated many of the terrible events that took place. Mladić had overall command of the troops who had laid siege on Sarajevo, and the UN units at Srebrenica and Zepa were from the Netherlands, the so-called 'Dutchbat'. A government-commissioned Dutch investigation into the management and behaviour of the Dutchbat units at Srebrenica resulted in the resignation of the prime minister in 2002, and controversies surrounding the massacre and its subsequent investigation (including suspicions surrounding the

whereabouts of a potentially incriminating roll of army film)
have continued to trouble political life in the Netherlands to
this day, reawakening difficult memories – histories – from the
Second World War.[19]

Magic

Throughout the 1960s, Amsterdam was a centre of the
European counter-culture: the realm of the so-called 'magic
apple', a haven for hippies, wanderers, and avant-gardistes –
and the site of political demonstrations and some riots. In *The
Spirit of the Time/De tijdgeest* (1968, 42 min.), Van der Keuken
configures the complexities of the city's contemporary history
into a documentary collage, a rendering that is artistically –
if not always uncritically – sympathetic to the experimental,
counter-cultural mood of the times.

The film is structured by a series of dialectically juxtaposed sequences and abstract images. It opens with footage
of a large group of conservatively dressed, and predominantly
middle-aged and older citizens walking under banners declar-
ing their support for the US government and its involvement
in Vietnam. The several mounted policemen who accompany
this march are there to protect the marchers, who are demonstrating against a larger, nosier, and younger anti-government
protest. The film then cuts to a close, long, motionless shot of
a section of riveted girders (perhaps, the join in the structure
of a steel bridge), and then to an anti-Vietnam rally, this time
torch-lit and full of carnivalesque antics and political sloga-
neering, especially the controversial: 'LBJ ... Murderer!'.[20]
This sequence culminates with a freeze-frame of a young
man whose head is bleeding badly, and who has doubtless
just been struck by one or more mounted policemen. (In
February 1968, the West German radical, Rudi Dutschke, led
a famous torch-lit anti-Vietnam demonstration through the
centre of Amsterdam, and this footage may well have been
taken at that particular event.) The film then cuts to a montage of abstract images (clouds, raindrops, a tree, and a field
of wheat swaying with the wind) and airy, celestial music, fol-

lowed by a montage of images of modernity and industry (the riveted girders, pylons, lorries, an airport runway, and new houses). In this introductory segment, pro-establishment and anti-establishment groups are shown as locked in conflict, as antithetical to one another as day and night, natural and industrial reality. The intercut images of the riveted girders evoke this sense of deadlock, as well as alluding to sculptures by the contemporary 'iron poet', Theo Niermeijer, whose work from this period offers witty, ironic perspectives on contemporary technology and industrial construction.

As with London in the 1960s, Amsterdam's 'spirit of the times' was as artistic as it was political, and Van der Keuken's film soon begins to explore the city's psychedelic subculture, and the role of LSD and other drugs. Motifs of magic, dreams, and hallucinations recur throughout the film, as do more abstract images, extreme facial close-ups, de-framings, special effects, and a free, noisy, a-synchronic soundtrack that includes a cacophony of children's high-spirited shouts and screams. Psychedelic culture is most obviously rendered in the sequences involving a contemporary Dutch rock band, Dragonfly. The hallucinatory experiences of the band members are imitated by Van der Keuken's cinematography and montage style, especially in one particularly surreal sequence in which a heavily made-up and bizarrely costumed member of Dragonfly goes to work as a clerk in an office, before 'mingling' in the street with pedestrians and shoppers. Again, the film relies on a pattern of juxtapositions, especially when the associations gather around a dream–reality dichotomy, where dreams are either hallucinogenic and mind-expanding, or socially utopian.

The most significant Amsterdam-based avant-garde movement of the 1960s was Provo (short for 'provocateurs'), and some of its leading lights and their antics influenced *The Spirit of the Time*. Provo was officially formed in May 1965, and its lifespan – like that of CoBrA – was short. Its immediate inspiration came from Jasper Grootvelt's 'happenings', although 'happenings' and situationist activities had been occurring in Amsterdam since the late 1950s. Despite his anti-smoking

6   *The Spirit of the Time/De tijdgeest*

'happenings', however, Grootvelt (a chain-smoker, himself) did not formulate a clear ideological focus and purpose for the movement; the nature of the provocation mattered more than any of its political objectives. Like Lucebert, Grootvelt was inspired by Johan Huizinga's *Homo Ludens: A Study of the Play-Element in Culture/Homo Ludens: Proeve Ener Bepaling Van Het Spelelement Der Cultuur* (1938), and he championed the notion of play for play's sake, and the second coming of *homo ludens*. Interestingly, Nieuwenhuys also joined the ranks of Provo, and used it as a platform for his theories about the New Babylon. Another key figure was Robert Stolk, who features in *The Spirit of the Time* working at his printing press, and joking around with Van der Keuken. If Provo did have a chief ideologue, however, it was Roel van Duijn, an anarchist who wrote manifestos for the movement. Despite van Duijn's best efforts, and a rhetorical patois that integrated anarchist, pacifist, and Marcusian terminology, 'the "Provo ideology" and the way it was presented', as Niek Pas has remarked, 'was perhaps

more a pop art than a serious contribution to social theory'.[21]
Even the environmental and social utility of Provo's successful
'white plan' projects – some of which exist in Amsterdam to
this day – was more inadvertent than deliberate.

The form of *The Spirit of the Time* emphasises the role of
multiple identities, parallel realities, and a plurality of per-
ceptions: images of doors and windows are ubiquitous
throughout the film. One sequence foregrounds the notion of
multiple Americas, for example, and features a man wearing
a cowboy hat watching a Hollywood western on television,
as Bob Dylan's 'I Dreamed I saw St. Augustine' plays in the
background. Another sequence involves the novelist and photographer, Ewald Vanvugt, enacting – through a montage of
made-up or masked facial close-ups – an experience he had
during an LSD trip when he imagined he was 'no longer one
particular human-being – but all humans throughout history'.[22]
In another remarkable episode, the performance poet-cum-
magician, Johnny van Doorn (aka 'Johnny the Self-Kicker')
hysterically recites a poem that fixates on dream lives, while
a sequence from the popular Dutch television comedy of the
period, *The Mounties* – in which one of the characters wakens
suddenly from a dream – is juxtaposed with news footage of
an astronaut space walking. Like Provo, the Living Theatre
collective was also committed to a loosely pacifist–anarchist
ideology, and both groups associated the use of drugs with the
creation of a collective consciousness, with actors often taking
LSD or smoking marijuana on stage, together with members
of the audience. In 1963, Julian Beck (who is listed in the cred-
its for *The Spirit of the Time*) and Judith Malina were forced
to temporarily decamp from New York to Europe, and they
kept the Living Theatre active through touring productions
in Belgium, France, Germany, and Italy, before taking up residence in Amsterdam, where Van der Keuken films the collective 'rehearsing' what appears to be an early version of *Paradise
Now*.

The moment of Provo was framed by two weddings. First,
in June 1965, it was announced that the heir to the throne,
Princess Beatrix of the Netherlands, had become engaged to

Claus von Amsberg, a German aristocrat who had served in the Wehrmacht, and whose family had enjoyed somewhat cordial relations with the Nazi regime. In the months during their engagement, Provo busied itself threatening to disrupt the royal wedding, and coordinating demonstrations and 'anti-Claus happenings' in Amsterdam. On the day of the ceremony, the jittery city authorities soon overreacted: a smoke bomb thrown from the crowd in the direction of the golden state coach precipitated a frantic, brutal response from the police. Second, in March 1969, John Lennon married Yoko Ono in Gibraltar. They had decided to spend their honeymoon staging 'Bed-ins' for peace. Hans Boskamp – a Dutch actor, socialite, and former international footballer – persuaded them to visit Amsterdam. The newlyweds duly took up residence in the Amsterdam Hilton. From their large white honeymoon bed in their large white hotel room, they held court before the world's press for a week. In keeping with the Provo enthusiasm for 'Bed-ins', 'Be-ins', and 'Smoke-ins', Lennon and Ono were presented with a 'white bike'. The 'White Bike Plan' was introduced by Provo in 1966, and although it was ostensibly designed to provide free bicycle transport, the idea had originally stemmed from a popular insult chanted at the royal couple at the time: 'Give me back my bicycle!' – a reference to the countless bicycles stolen by German soldiers as they hurriedly left Amsterdam at the end of the war. In mixing popular culture with politics, private space with mass media exposure, ultra-conventionality with utter absurdity, a Lennon–Ono 'Bed-in' was perhaps the last authentically counter-cultural 'happening' of the 1960s.

Photographs (1)

To Sang Photo Studio/To Sang Fotostudio (1997, 35 min.) was inspired by a 1995 photography book by Van der Keuken's friend, Willem van Zoetendael. Both men were fascinated by the working methods and personality of Li To Sang, a professional portrait photographer who had spent twenty years working from his small studio at 57 Albert Cuypstraat, in the

De Pijp district of Amsterdam. A long-time resident of that part of the city, Van der Keuken enjoyed its diverse, cosmopolitan communities, and daily market – reputed to be the busiest in the Netherlands.[23] In some respects, *To Sang Photo Studio* has a stronger claim to being a coda or epilogue to his *magnum opus*, *Amsterdam Global Village* (1996, 245 min.), than the more whimsical *Amsterdam Afterbeat* (1996, 16 min.): in *To Sang Photo Studio*, for example, the cultures of the world seem drawn – centripetally – into a tiny, cluttered space in the city, whereas in *Amsterdam Global Village*, the city is a more centrifugal phenomenon, a constant conduit between a here and an elsewhere.

The film depicts a series of visits to the studio, visits arranged by Van der Keuken, with each one involving a sitting for a portrait, and concluding with a shot of the finished photograph, unframed and set against a silk backdrop. To Sang is self-employed, and works in the studio with his wife, Ho Yuk Mui. Midway through the film, we learn that he was born and raised in China, travelled, studied art, and worked for a time in Surinam and Hong Kong. His ambition is to return to painting one day, referring to photography as 'a minor art'. The film's opening title sequence is a series of tracking shots of tramlines and shop fronts along Albert Cuypstraat, passing the market, a McDonald's restaurant, an ETOS store, and other shops, before cutting to a medium shot of To Sang peering out of his studio window onto the street. The first visitors to the studio are stylists working in a cosmetic wig shop, Hollywood Hair. Their visit is then followed by a Kurdish family who run a Turkish-Kurd restaurant; a Surinamese travel agent who is managing an office for Capricho Tours; two young women who work in the local supermarket; a Chinese woman who works in a Sang jewellery store (and who also came to the Netherlands from Suriname); and a Pakistani sari-maker and her elderly parents (who are visiting their daughter on a holiday). The film concludes with Van der Keuken – also a visitor to the photographer's studio – inviting To Sang and Yuk Mui to pose for a brief 'film-portrait'; hesitantly, they step into the frame, and sit for the camera, together.

Portrait photography would seem to be antithetical to street photography, and To Sang certainly appears to devote all his time directing and choreographing his subjects or models. In this so-called 'minor art', staging and composition is everything, and To Sang's instructions are gently authoritative, and his elegant gestures more characteristic of a magician than a portraitist (although, these arts have much in common). Regardless of the meticulous preparations, the moment when the photograph is taken remains a spontaneous, unrepeatable event, and Van der Keuken's camera is quick to catch the visitors' slightly disorientated, or displaced, demeanour when the session ends, and suddenly, they are back in *their* reality.

To Sang's gestures are closely observed by his visitors, and in each case the subtle interactions between photographer and subject culminate in this sudden breaking of the spell. Van der Keuken films this process – or metamorphosis – by preceding each visit with a brief sequence in which the subjects are shown going about their daily business, and speaking to the camera about how they came to be living and working in Amsterdam. With the exception of the supermarket assistants, all the subjects are from other countries, and continents. The Kurdish restaurateurs discuss politics and the conflict at home between the Turkish government and the separatists, the sari-maker talks about her experiences as a refugee with a UN passport, and the wig stylist teases a customer about wanting to look like Angela Davis. From here, Van der Keuken follows them into the studio, as they meet To Sang and discuss the type of photograph they would like him to take. To enter this photographer's studio is to step into a world of performance, and make-believe, where the so-called art of the real – photography – is just another purveyor of fictions. Further emphasising this paradox – and the fact that Van der Keuken and To Sang, film and photography, are simultaneously kindred and contrary spirits – the making of *To Sang Photo Studio* was itself the subject of a documentary about Van der Keuken, *Living with Your Eye/Leven met je ogen* (Ramón Gieling, 1997, 55 min.), and – as the director of that film put it: 'To Sang photographs the model with his camera. Then there's Johan's film camera, and

7 *To Sang Photo Studio/To Sang Fotostudio*

then there's my camera. This already makes the question more complex: who films whom, and who photographs whom?'[24]

Photographs (2)

Photography and actual photographs also feature significantly in Van der Keuken's *Last Words: My Sister Yoka (1935–1997)/ Laatste woorden: Mijn zusje Joke (1953–1997)* (1998, 50 min.), a film that documents two conversations between the filmmaker and his terminally ill sister. A therapist at a Jellinek Addiction Clinic for many years, Yoka is candid with her brother about the successes and disappointments of her life: 'What I know and what I have done is good enough.' Enduring constant discomfort and pain as the cancer destroys her body, she talks hopefully about her daughters and her grandchild. Many of her reminiscences are generous, and she speaks triumphantly about her rediscovery of painting and music in later life, and the publication of her book on addiction therapies. She also

expresses a lingering resentment towards her parents who dis-
approved of her behaviour at times, and who had difficulty
accepting her unplanned pregnancy when she was 19. As the
favoured son, Van der Keuken is gently reminded that he too
was sometimes part of the problem she had to face.

She is happy to be filmed, and – if anything – seems appreciative of an opportunity to record her words and thoughts at
this time, to be making a cinematic memento for her brother,
and immediate family. As *Last Words* progresses, her illness
worsens and Van der Keuken signifies her death by simply
filming a photograph of her lying in her bed, wrapped in blan-
kets and bathed in warm light, eyes closed, as he wants to
remember her. It is an image of an image, and his hand adjusts
it and he briefly caresses its surface with his fingertips. This
sequence also formed part of Van der Keuken's multimedia
exhibition, *From the Body to the City*, which first opened at
Maison Européenne de la Photographie in 1998, and which
developed directly from his interest in 'the interaction between
photography and film and where the two can viably coincide'.[25]
The film then concludes with a montage of snapshots and photographs of Yoka, beginning with images of her in her later
years, then as a younger woman, teenager, child, and baby in
a pram. Some of the images are taken from Van der Keuken's
first photography books, *We Are 17/Wij zijn 17* (1955), and
Behind Glass/Achter Glas (1957), and are the subject of a sharing
of histories between the brother and sister earlier in the film.
Possibly, this return to his photographs also indicates nostalgia for the solidity and apparent stability of youth in the face of
such a profound encounter with the certainty of death.

The film's opening sequence and the conversation with
Yoka's twin daughters, Elsie and Barbara, is also interesting
to consider in terms of Van der Keuken's style and its availability to experiences of loss and mourning. The film begins
with a medium close shot of flowers in Yoka's garden. The
colours and summer sunlight evoke a picturesque scene, an
image of life, growth, and beauty. As Van der Keuken's hand-
held camera then pans right, it stops and allows a window-
frame to obstruct the shot. It moves again and repeats this

deframing gesture, although this time the other side of the image is affected. It then pans through a door and into the sitting room where a conversation then begins. Later, when Yoka mentions her grown-up daughters, the film cuts to a very long take in which the camera simply films each daughter separately. Elsie stands on a balcony above a rehearsing orchestra (her workplace). The take includes her trying to find the right moment to begin speaking, shuffling a little and composing herself, waiting before she says something about her mother's illness. Once she has finished talking, the camera slowly pans right and leaves her behind: *temps mort*. Similarly, in the case of Barbara and her daughter, there is another long take that seems not to begin in any formal sense and only ends when the little girl shows off one of her paintings (of a zebra). These sorts of sequences are not unusual in Van der Keuken's work (e.g. *The Way South, Flat Jungle/De platte jungle* (1978, 90 min.), *Sarajevo Film Festival* (1993), and *To sang fotostudio* (1997)), and they convey that reticence in the face of reality that is – as Bergala insists – a key characteristic of his visual style. In this film, these sequences articulate a sense that there is nothing and everything to be said. Despite these gestures, however, *Last Words: My Sister Yoka* is perhaps, more Yoka's film than Van der Keuken's, as much her final self-portrait as his sympathetic, careful portrayal of his sister's experience of dying, and his experience of her death: 'We are motivated both by a strong desire to meet and make contact, and at the same time by an absolute horror of meeting someone else.'

Last things

The Long Holiday/De grote vakantie (2000, 145 min.) is Van der Keuken's last completed film, produced a year before his death, and an oblique remake of his 1974 film, *The Filmmaker's Holiday/Vakantie van de filmer*.[26] In 1998, Van der Keuken was again diagnosed with a cancer; his first illness had occurred in the mid 1980s, and the medical opinion now was that the latest tumour was manageable but incurable. In making *The Long Holiday*, he was also emulating something Van der Elsken

had done a decade earlier when – while also suffering from terminal prostate cancer: he made *Bye* (1990, VPRO, 108 min.).
Together with Noska van der Lely (and his stepson), Van der
Keuken headed off on a one-year trip to various countries and
places they had visited during their working lives together:
Nepal, Bhutan, Mali, Rio, San Francisco, and New York.
Travel had been an important aspect of their relationship, and
filming in faraway locations had provided Van der Keuken
with countless images and stories; often an idea for a film had
grown from a certain traveller's curiosity that then took him to
a place where the documentary would find its own story, deter-
mine its own structure and cinematic shape. In Amsterdam,
the world and its stories could even come to him.

By the end of the 1980s, Van der Keuken's first cancer diag-
nosis, the death of his sister, as well as that of other relations and close friends, and a general disillusionment with
the seemingly relentless march of neo-liberalism, led him to
reflect more deeply on the fragility of a life, and its ultimately
immeasurable legacy. However, in *The Long Holiday*, and *Last
Words: My Sister Yoka*, Van der Keuken's intimate experience
of terminal illness seemed to curtail formal experimentalism,
and, if anything, subordinate montage to the long take, and
the shot. *The Long Holiday*, for example, comprises sequences
shot on location in places with an intimate history, familiar
vista, or personal association. In so doing, its images seem to
chronicle – in a nearly diaristic form – a dying man's desire
to record the real, to keep or commemorate a representation
that is composed and continuous, stable and reliable – a post-
card from life, perhaps. As the film progresses, these sequences
alternate between those taken by Van der Keuken on his travels (and returns), and those taken on his visits to doctors and
oncologists. Even the film's impressionistic closing sequence
depicting boats and barges trafficking in a bay seems overly
photographic, and configured into a collection – rather than
a montage – of photographic images. Although this apparent
preference for the stillness and silence of photography appears
to turn the film towards a more conventional, realist documentary aesthetic, this tendency is also intercut at times by

figurative and self-consciously cinematic sequences, such as the extreme close shots of clinking porcelain teacups that symbolise home and companionship, as well as time, fragility, and fortune; and the sequence in which Van der Keuken 'remakes' Hitchcock's *Vertigo* in San Francisco as a love letter, using only a small video camera and a photograph of Van der Lely. The overriding impression, however, is that his film camera is trying to document the world, to frame it once and for all, and counter the passing of everything, and the loneliness of the self in the strange company of its own passing.

Notes

1 'the branded name'/'de getekende naam' (1952), trans. Diane Butterman, *Jacket Magazine*, October 2006, http://jacketmaga zine.com/31/nl-lucebert.html

2 See Jaap van der Bent, '"O Fellow Travellers I Write You a Poem in Amsterdam": Allen Ginsberg, Simon Vinkenoog, and the Dutch Beat Connection', *College Literature*, 27.1 (2000), pp. 199–212. Vinkenoog featured alongside other Beat figures (such as and Ginsberg, Corso, Anslem Hollo, Matthew Ferlinghetti, and William S. Burroughs) at the 1965 International Poetry Incarnation, held at the Royal Albert Hall, London. Although his performance is not included in Peter Whitehead's *Wholly Communion* (1965, b&w, 33 min.), it was one of the highlights of the IPI.

3 Andrew Hussey, 'Mapping Utopia: Debord and Constant Between Amsterdam and Paris', in *Paris–Amsterdam Underground: Essays in Cultural Resistance, Subversion, and Diversion* (Amsterdam: Amsterdam University Press, 2013), pp. 37–47; Peter Wollen, *Raiding the Icebox: Reflections on Twentieth Century Culture* (London: Verso, 1993), pp. 136–45.

4 Haanstra's *Glass/Glas* (1958), for example, won an Academy Award, and Van der Horst's *Keep It that Way!/Houen zo!* (1953) was awarded a short-film prize at the Cannes Film Festival, as was his *Praise the Sea/Prijs de zee* (1957) at the Berlin Film Festival. In 1958, Ivens's documentary *The Seine Meets Paris/ La Seine a rencontré Paris* – which was based around a script by Jacques Prévert – also won the short-film Palm d'Or at Cannes.

5 Van der Keuken's work has been the subject of several recent

studies: for example, Patricia Pisters, 'Form, Punch, Caress: Johan van der Keuken's Global Amsterdam', in *Imagining Global Amsterdam: History, Culture, and Geography in a World City'*, ed. Marco de Waard (Amsterdam: Amsterdam University Press, 2012), pp. 125–41; Renee Carine Hoogland, 'The Ambivalence of Visual Documentation: The Face in Johan van der Keuken', *Wide Angle*, 4.1 (2012): http://widescreenjournal.org/index.php/jour nal/article/view/124/176; Hing Tsang's 'Emotion, Documentary, and Van der Keuken's *Face Value'*, *Studies in Documentary*, 5.1 (2011), pp. 17–30.

6   See John Hess, *'I Love $*: An Avant-Garde Look at Money', *Jump Cut: A Review of Contemporary Media*, 34 (1989), p. 48. For a discussion of JVDK's political films from the 1960s and 1970s, see Cohn Chamber, 'Johan van der Keuken: Political and Experimental', *Jump Cut: A Review of Contemporary Media*, 34 (1989), pp. 41–7 . On the themes of displacement and refugee experience, see Hing Tsang's 'Christians, Moors, and Jews in the Work of Johan van der Keuken', *Interventions: International Journal of Postcolonial Studies*, 14.3 (2012), pp. 410–28.

7   Van der Keuken, 'Questions/Photographer and Filmmaker', 1999, www.moma.org/interactives/exhibitions/2001/jvdk/essays/essay1.html [accessed 03/09/2010].

8   Serge Daney, 'La radiation cruelle de ce qui est', *Cahiers du cinéma*, 290/291 (July/August 1978), pp. 69–72. For a critical engagement with Daney's article, see Thomas Elsaesser's 'The Body as Perceptual Surface: The Films of Johan van der Keuken', in his *European Cinema: Face to Face with Hollywood* (Amsterdam: Amsterdam University Press, 2003), pp. 198–211.

9   Bérénice Raynaud, 'Johan van der Keuken: Fragments for a Reflection', in *Border Crossing: The Cinema of Johan van der Keuken*, ed. Richard Herskowitz, exhib. cat. (Ithaca, NY: Herbert F. Johnston Museum of Art/Cornell University, 1990), p. 12.

10   Alain Bergala, 'On Photography as the Art of Anxiety', *Johan van der Keuken: The Lucid Eye: The Photographic Work, 1953–2000* (Amsterdam: De Verbeelding, 2001), p. 21.

11   François Albera, 'A Temporary World', *Johan van der Keuken: The Complete Collection: Volume 1* (DVD booklet), Arte Video, 2006, p. 7.

12   Serge Toubiana, 'Le monde au fil de l'eau: entretien avec Johan van der Keuken: *Amsterdam Global Village'*, *Cahiers du cinéma*, 517 (1997), p. 49. Trans. Lenny Borger as 'The Flow of the

World: Johan van der Keuken's *Amsterdam Global Village*', www. moma.org/exhibitions/2001/jvdk/general/general.htmlp [accessed 09/09/2010].

13   For an overview of this period, see Bob Moore, 'The Netherlands', in *The Oxford Handbook of Fascism*, ed. Richard Bosworth (Oxford: Oxford University Press, 2009), pp. 452–68. See also Dienke Hondius's study, *Return: Holocaust Survivors and Dutch Anti-Semitism* (Westport, CT: Praeger, 2003). Fons Rademakers's feature film *Like Two Drops of Water/Als twee druppels water* was also released in 1963, and also presents an uncompromisingly revisionist portrayal of Dutch resistance to the occupation.

14   On CoBrA, see Hal Foster, 'Creaturely Cobra', *October*, 141 (2012), pp. 4–21; Willemijn Stokvis, *Cobra: 1948–1951: A Return to the Sources of Art* (Zwolle, NL: Waanders, 2013).

15   Lucebert, *Collected Poems: Volume 1: 1949–1952*, trans. Diane Butterman (New York: Green Integer, 2010). See also Lucebert's *The Tired Lovers They Are Machines*, trans. Peter Nijmeijer (London: Transgravity Press, 1974).

16   He deploys the same hand-held framing technique in *De grote vakantie/The Long Holiday* (2000, NL, 142 min.) when filming from inside another Land Rover as the crew travel in Nepal.

17   Bergala, 'On Photography as the Art of Anxiety', *The Lucid Eye*, p. 25.

18   Bergala, 'On Photography', p. 25.

19   Thomas Elsaesser discusses the significance of several Dutch films dealing with the Bosnian conflict, and the legacy of Srebrenica, in his forthcoming, 'Paradoxes and Parapraxes: On (the Limits of) Cinematic Representation in Post-Conflict Situations', in *Post-Conflict Performance, Film, and Visual Arts: Cities of Memory*, eds Des O'Rawe and Mark Phelan (Basingstoke: Palgrave Macmillan, 2016). Radovan Tadic's documentary, *The Living and the Dead of Sarajevo/Les Vivants et les morts de Sarajevo* (1993, Fr., 75 min.), for example, might usefully be compared with *Sarajevo Film Festival Film*.

20   See Rimko van der Maar's '"Johnson War Criminal!" Vietnam War Protests in the Netherlands', in *Between Prague Spring and French May: Opposition and Revolt in Europe, 1960–1980*, eds Martin Klimke, Jacco Pekelder, Joachim Scharloth (Oxford: Berghan, 2011), pp. 103–15.

21   Niek Pas, 'Mediatization of the Provos: From a Local Movement

to a European Phenomenon', *Between Prague Spring and French May*, pp. 157–76.

22   Ewald Vanvugt, *Roofgoed Het Europees Museum van Overzee Gestolen Schatten*, http://ewaldvanvugt.wordpress.com/2013/04/16/the-spirit-of-the-time

23   *To Sang* (Amsterdam: Basalt, 1995). A graphic designer as well as a photographer, Van Zoetendael now collaborates with Nosha van der Lely in curating and exhibiting Van der Keuken's work.

24   Marcy Goldberg, 'In the Arena: Interview with Ramón Gieling', *Dox: Documentary Film Magazine*, 18 (1998), p. 18.

25   'I have been active for a good two decades in the border area between them, and have tried out any number of ways to link two or more photographs outside the ordinary chronological sequence. There are associations and contrasts pertaining to content, story, framework, composition, texture, colour, tone, movement and light. After these series of photographs came the "keyhole images" and the layered multiple exposures (Jaipur/India and Amsterdam/Two streets). What I wanted to do was confront these multiple photographs with moving pictures on film and video and find a different site for film: at some spot where people are walking around anyway, no longer confined to a seat in a movie theater, free to discover the images. A plan for seven exhibitions/installations on seven subjects emerged' ('Previous Exhibitions: 1998–1999', Maison Européenne de la Photographie, Paris, www.mep-fr.org/us/mois1.htm [accessed 21/06/2013]).

26   Van der Keuken was working on *For the Time Being/Onvoltooid tegenwoordig* (2002) when he died. The film – which is composed mainly of outtakes and short 'occasional' shots and sequences – was edited and released by Van der Lely as a ten-minute montage of friends talking about seemingly random topics, faces looking, and glimpses into other people's lives.

4

Eclectic dialectics

> We discover then that power is present in the most delicate
> mechanisms of social exchange: not only in the State, in classes,
> in groups, but even in fashion, public opinion, entertainment,
> sports, news, family and private relations, and even in the liber-
> ating impulses which attempt to counteract it. (Roland Barthes)[1]

As a documentary filmmaker, William Klein has been a
prodigious – if unpredictable – figure, often drawn to sensitive social fault lines, and the indeterminate spaces that exist
between conventional categories and histories of cinema. Like
Van der Keuken and Jean-Luc Godard, he belongs to a generation radicalised by the 1960s – and especially, the Vietnam
War – and his sensibility has little truck with received representations of reality. His film *œuvre* is varied and includes
documentaries on Muhammad Ali, May '68, Black Panthers,
professional tennis players, Little Richard, and Handel's
Messiah – as well as surrealistic satires on the fashion system,
French utopianism, and US culture and imperialism.

Although born in Brooklyn (in 1928), Klein settled in Paris
shortly after the Second World War to paint and study fine
art at the Sorbonne (under the occasional tutelage of Fernand
Léger). It was his photography, however, that initially earned
him an artistic reputation, and a living; his distinctive fashion
and street photographs from the 1950s and 1960s still exude an
edgy, intrusive aesthetic that combines formal iconoclasm with
social criticism. A steely executioner when it comes to taking a
photograph, Klein is more the wily interrogator when making
a film, where his documentary method has generally tended
towards a more cursory, essayistic method, probing the subject
matter rather than seizing on a dramatic revelation. Despite

this, his approach to both art forms is invariably underpinned
by discernible modernist tendencies: the disruption of familiar
distinctions (documentary/fiction, observation/participation,
vulgarity/sophistication, US/Europe); the incorporation of
displacements (chance, spontaneity, random juxtapositions);
and the foregrounding of ambiguity. In Klein's films, such
tendencies are always both aesthetically and politically significant, not least because they consistently subvert the rhetoric of
mainstream documentary.

Milieu/method

Klein is often portrayed as strictly independent and perma-
nently displaced – brash, abrasive, and difficult to deal with,
a windswept contrarian, refusing to identify with any cause
other than 'liberty and justice for all'.[2] Certainly, his film work
has never been readily assimilated into any particular school
or style of documentary, and it is surprising that his filmography is still relatively unacknowledged in studies of the documentary, especially in relation to discussions about Direct
Cinema, and how that movement might be distinguished from
classic *cinéma vérité*. While Klein's early Muhammad Ali documentaries, *Cassius, le grand* (1964, b&w, 42 min.) and *Float
Like a Butterfly, Sting Like a Bee* (1969, b&w, 94 min.), or his
Maydays/Grand soirs et petits matins (1968/1978, b&w, 97 min.),
for example, deploy observational techniques similar to those
of Robert Drew, Frederick Wiseman, D. A. Pennebaker, or the
Maysles brothers in their Direct Cinema heyday, his approach
is never faithful to some naive notion of rigorous objectivity
– oscillating, as it does, between assertion and speculation,
composition and reaction. Noël Burch even compares Klein's
'juxtaposition of still photographs with live shots in the same
scene' in *Float Like a Butterfly, Sting Like a Bee* with Godard's
'use of famous paintings as punctuation devices in his films'.[3]
Jonathan Rosenbaum, one of the few anglophone critics to
have written in any depth about Klein's work over the years,
has astutely remarked on how the Direct Cinema movement
was – for all its radical, countercultural kudos – constrained

by an attachment to forms that were conventional and journalistic, rather than inventive and artistic: 'This is a limitation happily unshared by Klein, whose anger, aggression, mockery, euphoria, volatility, and Punch 'n' Judy irreverence are never gratuitously slapped onto prosaic expositions but are emotional vectors that make new forms possible and necessary.'[4]

If anything, Klein's preference for hand-held tracking shots (that often culminate in a lingering wide-angle facial close-up), and ironic intercutting, sharp sense of metaphor, and his constant probing of how identities are invented and dramatised, might appear to bring his style closer to original *cinéma vérité*, and the so-called ethnofictions of a Jean Rouch (who, like Klein, was influenced by surrealism), or even the related works of Chris Marker (e.g. *The Lovely Month of May/Le joli mai*, with Pierre Lhomme, 1963, b&w, 163 min.). He may have been born and brought up in New York (and has done some of his best work there) but it was the experience of living and working in Paris – and the friendships that introduced him to various productions and people – that has had the most important influence on Klein's filmmaking style.

It was Marker, for example, who persuaded Éditions du Seuil to publish his photography book, *Life Is Good and Good for You in New York: Trance Witness Revels* (1956). Klein (and his late wife, Jeanne Florin) also feature as people from the future in Marker's *La Jetée* (1962, 27 min.), and his modulated voice can be heard narrating the English-language version of the film. He visited Rome and briefly worked with Fellini during the production of *Nights of Cabiria/Le notti di Cabiria* (1957). He was also recruited as the principal art designer on Louis Malle's *Zazie/Zazie dans le métro* (1960, 92 min.), where he met Philippe Noiret. At that time, Delphine Seyrig – who, like Noiret, would appear in Klein's *Who Are You, Polly Maggoo?/Qui êtes-vous Polly Maggoo?* (1966, b&w, 105 min.), and *Mr. Freedom* (1969, 105 min.) – was married to one of Klein's friends, Jack Youngerman, another US artist living in Paris. Interestingly, Seyrig's first film role was in Robert Frank and Alfred Leslie's *Pull My Daisy* (1958, b&w, 30 min.), which was shot in New York several months before Klein

made *Broadway by Light* (1959, 12 min.), his own first experimental short. Another important associate of Seyrig at this
time, Alain Resnais, is credited as the 'conseiller technique'
for *Broadway by Light*, and he and Marker were instrumental
in finding a producer for Klein's film (Anatole Dauman, no
less). In 1967, Klein contributed the US sequences to the anti-
war compilation film, *Far from Vietnam/Loin du Viêtnam* (1967,
120 min.), which was distributed by Marker's recently formed
Société pour le lancement des Œuvres Nouvelles (SLON), and
which also included work by Marker and Resnais, and Joris
Ivens, as well as Jean-Luc Godard, Michèl Ray-Gavras, Claude
Lelouch, and Agnès Varda. Klein's contribution to *Far from
Vietnam* was substantial; he provided extensive footage of anti-
war demonstrators in New York and an interview with the
family of Norman Morrison, who had committed suicide by
self-immolation in 1965, on the front lawn of the Pentagon (in
full view of Robert McNamara's office).[5] While Klein's work
may not have been especially important to the French New
Wave and *Cahiers du cinéma*, he was clearly involved with that
loose but more politically active ensemble of filmmakers, photographers, and writers who comprised the Left Bank Group.

Fashion/spectacle

Inevitably, New York street photography would sooner or
later become conventional despite itself, and be assimilated
into mainstream visual culture – and from there into banal-
ity. Inspired by wartime photojournalism, and encouraged by
the post-war surge in magazine sales, street photographers in
the 1950s resembled urban combatants, producing images that
belonged to the same heady cultural moment as free jazz, action
painting, and William S. Burroughs' *Naked Lunch* (1959). This
'anti-style' style also found its way into the fashion system,
where commodity fetishism is nothing to be ashamed of, and
glamour and grotesquerie can blithely inhabit the same aspect.

Klein's photography has been associated with numerous
fashion and lifestyle magazines, but it was his work with *Vogue*
in the 1950s and early 1960s that helped to establish his rep-

utation as a contemporary photographer of note. Recruited in 1954 by *Vogue*'s New York-based art director, Alexander Lieberman (who was also a relatively successful abstract artist and sculptor), Klein was initially commissioned by *Vogue* to complete a photographic diary of contemporary New York City. Although he was impressed by the originality of the resultant images, Lieberman thought them too hard-edged for the magazine's mainstream middle-class readership, encouraging Klein instead to concentrate on fashion photography, to direct his eye for incongruity to the choreographed world of couture and catwalks. For the next decade or so, his distinctive fashion photographs appeared regularly in *Vogue,* as well as other popular magazines, such as *Harper's Bazaar.*

Despite his cynicism towards the post-war proliferation of (US) lifestyle discourses, Klein embraced this opportunity to bring the language of fashion photography out into the street, to divest it of the formality and stylised austerity of an Irving Penn, or a Richard Avedon. With Klein behind the lens, models were often left to deal with whatever the city threw at them: hectic traffic, gawking passers-by, and unpredictable weather. In trying to capture the immediacy of the moment – what Roland Barthes refers to as fashion's 'absolute, dogmatic, vengeful present tense' – Klein dispensed with compositional conventions and deployed extreme shutter speeds, de-centrings, and unusual exposure and blurring techniques.[6] Coincidentally, the major fashion houses at this time were also in thrall to op art (i.e. optical-illusion art), and in many of Klein's iconic photographs from this period, dramatic contrasts and distortions are further accentuated by the solid geometry of op-inspired clothes designs.

By the 1960s, however, Klein had become increasingly interested in filmmaking. After *Broadway by Light,* he had made another twelve-minute colour short, *How to Kill a Cadillac* (1959), and five fifteen-minute packages for the French television current affairs series, *Front Page/Cinq colonnes à la une* (ORTF, 1962) including a reportage piece on the contemporary fashion industry, *The Fashion Business,* and *Department Stores/Aux grands magasins* (1963, b&w, 90 min.), which

featured Simone Signoret opining at length on the production
and retail of stylish clothes in Paris. His first feature-length
satire, *Who Are You, Polly Maggoo?*, was intended by Klein as a
deliberately discordant swan song to his career in fashion photography. One of the film's main characters, for example, Miss
Maxwell (Grayson Hall), is based on Diana Vreeland, *Vogue*'s
notorious editor-in-chief at the time. In the opening sequence,
Maxwell arrives at a fashion show to watch models (most notably, Donyale Luna) wearing grotesquely tailored aluminium
sheets that resemble Hugo Ball's 'cubist costume' from his
Cabaret Voltaire days. Amid the frantic press pack (and with
architects from *Utopie* milling around as extras),[7] and the sound
of loud, celestial choral music playing in the background, the
unfortunate models parade in front of Maxwell and her company of baying jurors and photographers. Although anchored
to a plot of sorts, *Who Are You, Polly Maggoo?* is closer to a
loosely constructed montage of incidents and non-sequiturs
(snap shots); the film includes fictional, nonfictional, and animated sequences and images (including some of Klein's own
fashion photographs and his other artwork).

The satirical subject of the film is not solely its eponymous
heroine (a fictitious US model working in Paris, played by a
real US model working in Paris, Dorothy MacGowan) and
the fashion system she serves. *Who Are You, Polly Maggoo?*
also satirises the contemporary fad for *actualité* television programmes documenting the lives of celebrities (Ed Murrow's
Person to Person series for CBS, for example). Throughout the
film, Polly is pursued by the crew from one such series (*Who
Are You …?*), and its besotted producer, Grégoire Pecque (Jean
Rochefort). No doubt, Klein interpreted the popularity of this
emergent television genre as symptomatic of how a genuinely
critical media was being replaced by one increasingly preoccupied with cultural trivia. Although his association with the
producers of *Front Page* had ended acrimoniously when his
feature-length film, *The French and Politics/Les français et la poli-
tique* (1962, ORTF, 90 min.) was censored, Klein valued cou-
rageous, politically intelligent filmmaking, and its role within
both the cinema and television.

Throughout the film, Polly Maggoo's life is depicted as cluttered and frenetic; nothing is predictable other than the caprice of her suitors, and the avarice of managers and producers. The fashion world, and its ensemble of models, divas, and hacks becomes a metaphor of the inanity of modern life – the film is full of ironic references to excess, decay (consumption), and death, and one of its most visually successful sequences is a fashion shoot, staged in a cemetery, at a mock funeral. The film also lampoons intellectuals, and any suggestion that fashion can lay claim to artistic credibility (with one character appearing as a sociologist of fashion, perhaps based on Barthes – who was writing on such topics at the time, and whose *Système de la mode/The Fashion System* was published in 1967). Combining modern fairytale (*Cinderella*), and allusions to popular news stories of the day (Prince Rainier and Grace Kelly, the Aga Khan and Sally Croker-Poole), fables, and gossip columns, *Who Are You, Polly Maggoo?* invokes the fashion world – where identities are at their most unstable, and reality, its most vulnerable – to create an allegory about the emptiness of appearances, the increasing irrelevance of journalism, and what to do about art that is not art.

When Klein returned to fashion photography in the 1980s, just as his earlier photographic work was being rediscovered by curators and critics, he was commissioned by TF1 (Télévision Française 1) to make a feature-length documentary on the 'new wave' of designers and models who were reasserting the international pre-eminence of Parisian couture, figures such as Jean-Paul Gaultier, Karl Largerfeld, Chantal Thomass, and Grace Jones. Although *Fashion in France/Mode en France* (1984, 98 min.) began life as a mainstream (promotional) production, it was not long before Klein began to play around with the original script, rethinking and restructuring the entire project.

The film opens with a prologue: a brief history of fashion, enacted by three models who change into different costumes signifying the different periods in this history, a history of revolutions and counter-revolutions, epochs of excess followed by austerity; in other words, it is a history of modern France told through fashion. There then follows a dozen sequences that resituate the film's cast of real-life designers and models in different cinema and television genres (documentary, film noir, slapstick, romantic comedy). Throughout, *Fashion in France* renders the relationship between performance and play as a *tableau vivant* of bodies and costumes, an impromptu theatre: Jean-Paul Gaultier dresses shoppers at a Paris market in ludicrous costumes, before sending them back onto the street; in another comic sketch, agnès b. spurns the advances of a would-be lover trying to seduce her with his sophisticated fashion-speak; Grace Jones and Linda Spierring improvise scenes from Marivaux's *The Game of Love and Chance*; and a peep show features Chantal Thomass and others proffering humorous clichés in the form of confessions about life and love, desire and disappointment. In satirising both the fashion world, in general, and its own pretentious documentary style, *Fashion in France* shares much with *Who Are You, Polly Maggoo?*

Body/motion

The subject of fashion photography is never solely clothes or costuming; it also represents bodies, faces, gestures, and reactions. Klein's interest in the human body, and how it moves and transforms the space around it, might also owe something to Léger, whose art and writing often deals with puppetry, masks, animation, and mechanical objects; *Ballet mécanique* (1924, 19 min.), which he co-directed with Dudley Murphy, being an interesting point of reference in this context. In *Slow Motion/Ralentis* (1984, 30 min.), Klein filmed the movements of various bodies; using a specially designed 35 mm camera, he filmed athletes from fifteen Olympic sports going through their paces. The film, perhaps, owes more to the famous human locomotion studies of Eadweard Muybridge and Étienne-Jules Marey than *Ballet mécanique*, drawing attention both to the anatomical components of athletic motion, and the individual frames – or *photographic* components – of cinema, itself.

In a later film, *Babilée '91* (1992, b&w, 57 min.), Klein carefully observes the movements of the body by paying homage to the dancer and choreographer, Jean Babilée, as he prepares for a new production of *Life*, a modern ballet originally composed and choreographed for him by Maurice Béjart in the late 1970s. *Life* involves only two dancers (a man and a woman), who interact with and manipulate a large, lightweight rectangular frame, constantly changing and reframing space and movement. *Babilée '91* is only incidentally interested in the opening night performance of *Life* at the Théâtre des Champs-Élysées. Shot entirely in black and white, with minimal sound and editing, Klein's film comprises a series of sequences in which the 62-year-old Babilée exercises, rehearses, and ruminates on his performance in the original production of the ballet (while watching an old video recording of that performance), sequences in which Klein hopelessly tries to separate the dancer from the dance. Babilée is a master performer in every sense, and if Klein's film discovers anything about him it is his otherworldly, or curiously angelic, quality – as he deftly scoots through the streets of Paris on his motorbike, or dances into his own past. However, in considering what is formally distinctive about Klein's documentary method, it is useful to contrast *Babilée '91* with another film about this subject, Patrick Bensard's *Le Mystère Babilée* (2000, Fr., 90 min.), a conventional television documentary that succeeds only in making the real Babilée disappear altogether.

The relations between fashion and choreography, spectacle and performance, photography and cinema are also integral to *The French* (1981, 130 min.), Klein's feature-length documentary on the French Open at Roland Garros. In the 1980s, professional tennis, like the fashion system, was still more a transatlantic than a global phenomenon. Tennis was also a sport synonymous with style and sartorial elegance (nowadays, names such as Fred Perry, René Lacoste, and Bjorn Borg are more readily associated with colourful menswear than centre-court heroics). In *The French*, Klein films the athletic, commercial, and social aspects of the tournament: from the organisers' preparations to pre-tournament training and physiotherapy sessions, changing-room banter between the players, the busy commentary boxes, and lavish receptions for sponsors

and businessmen. The film often catches its celebrity athletes
unawares, as they kill time before and between matches, often
discussing the strengths and weaknesses of potential opponents. In these situations, Klein's hand-held, cursory style
seems free and available to any opportunity (and personality)
that happens to present itself. Claire Clouzot has remarked on
this technique in the film: 'The "Klein-touch" is a combination of sympathy, voyeurism, and jubilation. Everyone knows
they are being filmed ... and they address this visible–invisible
man without ceremony.'[8] Until the film's finale, excerpts
from the matches are kept brief, merely intercutting from the
main event: the function of the tournament and its players in
enhancing corporate hospitality and maintaining or attracting
new major sponsors. In the sequences from the latter stages of
the tournament, especially the men's singles final, however,
Klein changes the aesthetic, alternating hand-held cinematography with languid, slow-motion shots of the players in action
during rallies, as if indulging a romantic admiration for their
skill by replacing the hitherto jerky, observational framing
with something stylised to represent the beauty of human athleticism, and its capacity to transcend the trivia and circus
commercialism associated with televised professional sport
in modern society. These sequences anticipate *Slow Motion*,
where Klein abstracts the phenomenon of human athleticism
from its competitive and commercial context, the gesture from
the spectacle. Both *Slow Motion* and *The French* also suggest
similarities between certain sports and the cinema; for Serge
Daney, for example, tennis is 'the *same thing* as cinema, or at
least an older cinema, that of *mise en scène* and topography ... it
wouldn't take much effort for me to find passing-shots in Fritz
Lang and inserts with Miroslav Mecir'.[9]

This climax to *The French* is made all the more effective by
the antics of John McEnroe in a previous sequence, upbraiding
the French umpire during his semi-final match against Ivan
Lendl. Given Klein's interest in the contradictions between
behaviour and reality, performance and authenticity, US and
Europe, McEnroe is certainly a suitable case for documentary
treatment. Patriotically sporting a gaudy US Davis Cup track-

suit, he is also a peculiar kind of rebel, whose gripes about the weather, the umpire, the tournament referee, and everyone else who seems to be conspiring to sabotage his chances of winning the tournament, appear to issue from a typical anti-authoritarian temperament. However, McEnroe's clown-like appearance, eccentric mannerisms, and argumentative disposition belie an astute tactician whose rage for justice is perhaps just a strategy to attract attention, and distract his opponent.

In general, however, the style of filmmaking in *The French* minimises the pretence of objectivity. Although structured by fourteen 'chapters', for example, the film contains no voice-over narration, or direct interviews (although players and officials are sometimes filmed giving interviews to others (that is, filmed being filmed), and, occasionally, even asking Klein to stop filming. In a 2001 interview, published in *L'Équipe*, Jean-Luc Godard bemoaned how television directors overuse close-ups and gimmicky slow-motion techniques when filming sport: 'They're not looking for the truth of things, they're looking for the glory of the event. They want to bowl viewers over. They inhabit the camera, take it over like squatters, but the spirit of the camera doesn't inhabit them, nor does sport.'[10] Godard might approve of Klein's approach, which contrasts with this kind of sensationalist style, and which refuses to allow the 'glory of the event' to overwhelm 'the truth of things'. This technique is similar to that deployed throughout *Muhammad Ali: The Greatest/Le Combat au Zaïre* (1974, 120 min.), a quasi-compilation film that has a first part which includes sequences from earlier black-and-white documentaries made by Klein on the eve – and aftermath – of Ali's victory over Sonny Liston, *Cassius, le grand* (1964, b&w, 100 min.), and *Float Like a Butterfly, Sting Like a Bee* (1969, b&w, 94 min.), and a second part dealing with Ali's 1974 world-title fight against George Foreman. Klein was first introduced to Ali after a chance meeting with Malcolm X, on a plane in 1964. He was soon given permission to film Ali and his entourage of family, friends, trainers, sparing partners, and wealthy (white) 'owners' (the Louisville Syndicate) in the run-up to the fight against Liston. Like *The French*, the ostensible subject of the film (Ali's Big Fights) is often displaced by the more mundane *dispositif* that envelops 'the glory of the event'.[11]

Just as *The French* is a film about gifted athletes playing tennis, and the insatiable commercialisation of that sport, so too *The Greatest* is both a film about a remarkable boxer, his charismatic personality, and his particular relationship to racial politics and civil rights. Ali's management team – as opposed to his trainers – are introduced at the beginning of the film in sinister chiaroscuro; they regard his conversion to Islam as 'ingratitude', and the atmosphere in the film often smoulders with contempt and the stench of casual racism. Similarly, in one especially memorable sequence before Ali's bout against Liston, a room full of white managers and officials argue over how much notice is required before publically announcing the name of the fight referee; again, the world of regulations and decisions is also the world of racial privilege. Throughout the film, Ali invariably speaks *at* the camera, in medium shot or close-up, often glowing in the strong sunlight. Similarly, Malcolm X, in one sequence, is framed in medium close-up, impassioned and impressive. Orator, poet, stand-up comic, and preacher, Ali speaks endlessly; he mesmerises his audience, ridiculing his opponents, and the white impresarios and politicos seeking to exploit his talent.

In the second part of the film, a decade has elapsed and the all-conquering Cassius Clay is now Muhammad Ali trying to win back his world title from Foreman. The bout (the legendary 'Rumble in the Jungle') is being held in Zaire and not the US, as the grainy black-and-white cinematography of *Cassius, le Grand* becomes the vivid Eastman colours of *The Greatest*. The event was saturated in irony: Don King and a consortium of (mainly, English) promoters arranged the event with representatives of President Mobutu, who was keen to host the fight and put up the multimillion dollar purse. Mobutu, of course, was a byword for despotism and corruption, and had been instrumental in the murder of Patrice Lumumba in 1962 (Lumumba was a hero of Malcolm X). This context is implicit in the film, and Ali's attempts to transcend it by identifying with Africa as his homeland is emphasised, while the adulation of the Kinshasa crowds recalls the children singing songs about him in the shantytowns of Florida and Atlanta at the beginning of *Cassius, le Grand*. In *The Greatest*, Klein again holds two themes in tandem: on the one hand, this is a film about athleticism, and its participants and fans; and on the other, it is about a culture of greed, and exploitation. Just as Klein was fascinated by designers and models but nauseated by the fashion system they served, so too, throughout *The Greatest*, he configures the language of documentary film to celebrate athleticism and theatricality while also exposing the profiteering and political skulduggery that invariably accompany such spectacles. Klein's fascination with sport and its phenomenology, like that of fashion, again resonates in the writings of Barthes:

> At certain periods, in certain societies, the theatre has had a major social function: it collected the entire city within a shared experience: the knowledge of its own passions. Today it is sport that in its way performs this function. Except that the city has enlarged: it is no longer a town, it is a country, often even ... the whole world; sport is a great modern institution cast in the ancestral forms of spectacle.[12]

Politics/performance

Throughout the 1960s, Ali's popularity contributed to the development of African-American political consciousness. His conversion to Islam and change of name, not to mention his much-publicised associations with well-known reformist and militant activists added to his counter-cultural credentials, as did his refusal to be conscripted in 1967. By the mid 1980s, however, Ali had become an ornament of the establishment, supporting Ronald Reagan's re-election campaign. Meanwhile, the Black Panthers' former Minister of Information, Eldridge Cleaver, was attempting to accomplish an even more unlikely ideological summersault, becoming a born-again Christian, and then a Mormon, a member of the Republican Party, and another surprise convert to Reaganism. Klein's *The Greatest* and *Eldridge Cleaver: Black Panther* (1970, col., 80 min.) were

produced at a time (or times, in the case of Ali) when both
men were at their radical, and rhetorical, best. Neither film
explicitly challenges their political commitments but Klein's
preference for unsteady, scanning facial close-ups of Cleaver
(in contrast to his framing of Malcolm X) does reveal moments
when the subject suddenly makes himself untrustworthy,
when the camera's patient scrutiny allows something contradictory to leak out into the *mise en scène*, and an impassioned
speech suddenly becomes the performance of a performance.

Not long after achieving independence in 1962, Algeria
sought to consolidate its identity as a model of national liberation and pan-African solidarity. In 1969, Cleaver had become
persona non grata in Cuba (where he had fled after jumping
bail in December, 1968), and he was then taken to Algeria by
Cuban diplomats, to be reunited with his heavily pregnant
wife, Kathleen. As one of the party's most recognisable figures, he was also anxious to generate much-needed political
and financial capital, and stumbling upon the inaugural Pan-
African Festival in Algiers, he quickly realised its potential in
promoting the Panther cause, and establishing new alliances.
Klein also came to Algeria in 1969; thanks to his involvement in the *Far from Vietnam* project, the Algerian government
invited him to direct *The Pan-African Festival of Algiers* (1969,
90 min.). The Pan-African festival film was also a compilation,
and the Algerians were keen to recruit sympathetic international directors to assist in publicising the festival, and the
achievements of the newly liberated nation.[13] Cleaver appeared
in the film along with other members of the Black Panther
delegation; he then approached Klein directly, and asked him
to make a second film (also funded by the Algerians) about his
work there, and hopes for political revolution in the US.

Originally entitled *The State of the Union*, *Eldridge Cleaver:
Black Panther* was shot over three days, and comprises sequences
in which Cleaver explains the policies of the Panthers, his
hostility to the US government, and the violence of racism,
capitalism, and imperialism. In keeping with Klein's tendency
to incorporate images from other media forms (especially, television) into his documentaries, these interviews are intercut

(often without interrupting Cleaver's well-honed diatribe) with newsreel footage, photographs, newspaper cuttings, and shots of him visiting the North Vietnamese embassy, or strolling around the Kasbah (shopping for a flick-knife), freedom fighter-cum-*flâneur*. In one episode from the film, entitled 'Language', Cleaver justifies his frequent use of obscene language: it is a political act, violating the culture of the oppressor ('the pigs'), who insist on 'Oxford English' as a means of excluding the poor and the powerless from politics. Television news footage of Reagan arriving and departing from LAX airport, and being interviewed by journalists, is accompanied by a soundtrack from a rally in which Cleaver is exhorting the crowd to chant repeatedly: 'Fuck Ronald Regan!' (Reagan had refused Cleaver a permit to teach in any university or college in the state of California, and was the object of his considerable ire throughout the late 1960s and early 1970s). In the latter parts of the film, Klein's intercutting techniques shift the emphasis away from Cleaver, and towards a much wider political context. It is not that Cleaver disappears from *his* film, but the inclusion of montage sequences of newsreel and still photographs (especially, relating to the Vietnam War) displaces his rhetoric, shifting attention away from this individual, and his charismatic appearance.

Klein's relationship with political filmmaking dates back to the controversy over *The French and Politics*, and his pop-art-inspired satire on US foreign policy and Vietnam, *Mr. Freedom*. In 1978, he also released *Maydays/Grands soirs et petits matins* (16 mm, 97 min.), an observational documentary made up entirely of footage shot during some of the events that took place in Paris in 1968, or 'Mai '68 au Quartier latin'. In discussing this film, Alison Smith comments that much of it 'resembles an album of photographs in which we are shown not merely the photographs themselves, but also the process of selecting them out of the chaos of the surrounding reality'.[14] This mode of construction is not only consonant with the film's hand-held style, it also complements Klein's tendency towards the ironic: as well using elliptical inter-titles, *Maydays* (like *The French*) is introduced with ragtime piano music, has no voice-over

8 *Eldridge Cleaver: Black Panther*

narration, and seems to just happen upon various surrealistic images and associations. Paris has become an open parliament, a crucible of debate, manifestoes, committees, revolutionary fervour, and direct action against the state. Again, without fixating on (or criticising) the political leaders of the protests, *Maydays* registers something significant about the heterogeneous and theatrical nature of popular politics at this time. Despite its own political sympathies, the film's form – its loose structure and cursory style – also reflects its main theme: the fragility of the alliance between workers and intellectuals, and the capability of the state to regulate radical politics, and dilute dissent.[15]

Religion/music

In the late 1970s, Klein made a trilogy of 16 mm documentaries exploring aspects of contemporary US culture and society: *Hollywood, California: A Loser's Opera* (1977, 60 min.), *Music*

9   *Maydays/Grands soirs et petits matins*

City, US (1978, 75 min.), and *The Little Richard Story* (1980, 90 min.). Popular music and show business are important motifs in this odyssey through the dusty hinterlands of the American Dream, and so too is the Puritan personality, and the incendiary moments when the politics of race, religion, and capital coincide. Although the films explore issues familiar to the Direct Cinema tradition – the Maysles brothers' *Salesman* (1968, b&w, 85 min.), or even their *Meet Marlon Brando* (1966, b&w, 28 min.), for example – Klein, of course, does not share the belief that observation can ever be objective, reliable, and an end in itself.

The Little Richard Story, for example, begins as a documentary about Little Richard's life in the late 1970s. The once self-proclaimed 'Queen of Rock 'n' Roll' – who, interestingly, never had a number one hit in the US – has *again* become a born-again Christian, dedicating his life to Gospel music, while endorsing expensive Black Heritage bibles. It is clear – even from what little we see of him in the film – that Little

Richard is psychologically brittle, and Klein is careful not to
caricature him too readily. At any rate, the singer only makes
brief appearances, and generally in the form of intercut footage
from old television shows, or – more uncannily – in the costumes and performances of his legion of impersonators (many
of whom look nothing like him). One sequence finds Little
Richard sitting behind a desk in the offices of Memorial Bibles
International, wearing a business suit, and singing 'The Saints'.
He proves an unreliable and elusive subject, failing to attend a
Little Richard Day organised in Macon, Georgia, to celebrate
his life. Even here, however, Klein's eye for irony does not
disappoint, as the white Mayor of Macon gives an excruciating
rendition of 'I Left My Heart in San Francisco' to the crowd,
a song generally associated with Italian-American crooners
like Tony Bennett, Perry Como, and Frank Sinatra. Another
sequence in the film, involves a long travelling shot – taken
from the back of a moving car – of the run-down, impoverished
parts of Macon – the world of Little Richard's childhood, and
of his aunt who still lives there, and who proudly shows Klein
photographs of the young star in his Gospel-singing days. If
Little Richard invented rock 'n' roll, then, so too did Gospel
music, and the references to this background are made explicit
in the local church where a choir of women are filmed singing
and dancing, which is also a gesture of defiance, an occasion of
freedom.

As Richard's relationship with his (white) employers at
Memorial Bibles breaks down, he absconds (on God's advice,
he claims), leaving Klein to improvise the rest of his film. In
fact, it is the absence of Little Richard that becomes increasingly significant. The disappearing, or displaced, subject –
whose image is then fragmented into other media images – is
after all a recurrent trait in Klein's work, and is consistent
with a documentary method that does not so much accost the
unpredictable as actively seek it out. Little Richard's story is
displaced by other stories – and by what Rosenbaum describes
as those 'emotional vectors that make new forms possible and
necessary'. This film becomes a documentary about people
who desire to be Little Richard, and also a film about the

condition of America in 1980, especially in those economically desolate towns and cities of the South.

The Little Richard Story is consistent with Klein's broader interest in the relationship between sporting or musical (cultural) achievement and wider social questions, probing the underside of fame, glamour, and consumerist hype. It is an example of his fascination with individuals whose life (and lifestyle) embodies the contradictions of their times. Handel's *Messiah*, however, seems to offer no such immediate social context, and it is not obvious what attracted Klein to this project in the first place, to the task of rendering a musical celebration of Christian liturgy into the language of documentary film. One of the hallmarks of Klein's style, however, has been his use of ironic intercutting. This technique often functions to widen a film's thematic and political contexts, to create critical space for a more imaginative form of documentary engagement. In this sense, the architecture of Handel's oratorio offers a surprising array of 'inter-cutting' possibilities. For example, *Messiah* is divided into three parts. The first comprises five scenes relating to prophecies and expectations, the nativity, and the ministry of Christ. The second part is made up of seven scenes encompassing Christ's passion, death, and resurrection. The third contains four scenes that celebrate the triumph of righteousness over evil, love over money, an eternity of peace and goodwill under the reign of the Messiah. Each scene comprises movements, and there are over fifty of these in the entire oratorio, each based on biblical quotations. The relationship between the movements conforms to a logic or rhetorical shape not dissimilar to that of dialectical montage, progressing from a recitative 'cell' to an aria, and culminating in a chorus (most famously in this case, the Hallelujah chorus).

Klein's film is assembled from short live-action and staged sequences, newsreel clips, photographs, religious paintings, and so on. This stream of images is inter-cut throughout by sequences from a live studio performance of *Messiah* by Les Musiciens du Louvre (Grenoble), conducted by Marc Minkowski. Throughout, Klein's images relate ironically or associatively to the original meaning and emotion of the

movement they accompany; and different professional and
amateur choirs and vocalists (mainly, from the US) are filmed
singing the various movements. For example: Movement 7
(1.2), 'He Shall Purify the Sons of Levi' is sung by the New
York-based Lavender Light People of All Colors Lesbian and
Gay Choir, while Movement 22 (2.1), 'Behold the Lamb of God
that Taketh Away the Sins of the World' is sung by the Dallas
Police Department Choir. Las Vegas and its casinos feature
prominently in the film ('Behold Your God!'), as do images
from the first Gulf War ('Nativity'), and sites of religious conflict, such as the Middle East, Kashmir, Bosnia, and Northern
Ireland. Other sequences were shot at large religious festivals
and gatherings (for example, the Passion play at Iznájar, the
March for Jesus at Houston, Texas), and many highlight the
kitsch and surreal aspects of evangelical Christianity in
the US, such as an event organised by a group calling themselves 'Bodybuilders for Christ', or the billboard advertisement
for a Christian road haulage company: 'Transport for Christ:
Reclaiming a Dynamic Gospel for a Dynamic Industry'.
Klein's *Messiah* wagers on compatibilities between opposites
(the classical and the kitsch, the sacred and the profane, fictions and documents), on creating provocative juxtapositions,
and maintaining – in its own distinctive fashion – that essential dialectic between art and politics.

Behind the irony, subjectivity, and wit, there is always a gen-
erosity in Klein's documentary filmmaking towards disparate
influences, and an irrepressible curiosity about the mystery
of reality. Klein himself would probably prefer to put these
qualities down to simple intuition, and a version of what Orson
Welles liked to call 'the confidence of ignorance'. However,
the variety and serendipity of subject matter across his *œuvre*
is as much a product of a deliberate method as a consequence
of chance, or a photographer's instinct for the opportune. A
one-time protégé of Dada, Klein has always appreciated the
expressive potential of improbable juxtapositions, of intercutting between times and places, and subverting mainstream
journalistic forms and strategies. This attitude remains rare
among contemporary documentary filmmakers, and yet it is

the very quality that gives Klein's work a distinctive aesthetic texture, and relevance to any history of documentary film.

Notes

1   Roland Barthes, 'Lecture in Inauguration of the Chair of Literary Semiology, Collège de France, January 7, 1977', trans. Richard Howard, *October*, 8 (1979), p. 4.

2   Klein used this phrase in a 2009 Regis Dialogue with Paulina del Paso, at the Walker Arts Centre, www.walkerart.org/channel /2009/william-klein-regis-dialogue-with-paulina-del   [accessed 07/07/2012].

3   Noël Burch, *Theory of Film Practice*, trans. Helen R. Lane (New York: Praeger, 1973), p. 61.

4   Jonathan Rosenbaum, 'Documentary Expressionism: The Films of William Klein', *Cinema Outsider*, exh. cat. (Minneapolis: Walker Art Center, 1989), p. 20. See also Katherine Dieckmann's 'Raging Bill: William Klein's Films', *Art in America*, 78.12 (1990), pp. 71–6. More recently, critics such as Adrian Martin and David Campany have written on Klein's filmmaking and its relations to other aspects of his artistic career. See Martin's 'William Klein: Waiting for a Photographer' (Australian Centre for the Moving Image, 2008), www.acmi.net.au/william_klein_essay. htm [accessed 04/01/2014], and Campany's 'William Klein's Way', *William Klein: ABC* (London: Tate/Abrams, 2012).

5   The tendency to marginalise Klein's contribution to this film (and the Left Bank group, and its politics) is not unusual. For example, see Thomas Waugh's '*Loin du Vietnam* (1967), Joris Ivens, and Left Bank Documentary', *Jump Cut: A Review of Contemporary Media*, 53 (2011), www.ejumpcut.org/archive/jc53. 2011/WaughVietnam/3.html [accessed 02/12/2013].

6   Roland Barthes, *The Language of Fashion* (London: Berg, 2006), p. 116.

7   Jean-Louis Violeau, 'Artists and Architects in May 1968: An Aesthetics of Disappearance', in *May '68: Rethinking France's Last Revolution*, eds Julian Jackson, Anna-Louise Milne, and James S. Williams (Basingstoke: Palgrave Macmillan, 2011), p. 268.

8   Claire Clouzot, *William Klein: Films* (Paris: Maison Européenne de la Photographie, 1998), p. 18.

9   Serge Daney, *Postcards from the Cinema*, trans. Paul Douglas Grant (Oxford: Berg, 2007), p. 83.

10   Jean-Luc Godard, *The Future(s) of Film: Three Interviews: 2000–01*, trans. John O'Toole (Bern: Verlag Gachnang and Springer, 2002), pp. 74–5.

11   In this respect, *Muhammad Ali: The Greatest* also calls to mind Norman Mailer's book, *The Fight* (New York: Little, Brown, 1975). For a useful overview of *Muhammad Ali: The Greatest*, incorporating an interview with Klein, see Steve Gravestock's 'Exiled on Main Street: William Klein on *The Greatest*', *Cinemascope*, 14 (2003), pp. 23–6. According to Klein's cinematographer on *Cassius le grande*, Étienne Becker (another associate of Chris Marker who had worked on both *La jetée* (1962, b&w, and *Le joli mai* (1963, b&w, 157 min.)), *Cassius le grande, Sting like a Butterfly* is itself a compilation of three earlier short documentaries: *Cassius le grande, La grande hernie* (1964), *Le grande homme* (1965).

12   Barthes, *What Is Sport?*, trans. Richard Howard (New Haven, CT: Yale University Press, 2007), pp. 57–9. *What Is Sport?* was written in 1960 as a script for a Canadian documentary, *Le sport et les hommes*, directed by Hubert Aquin. In 1961, Barthes also collaborated with Michel Brault on another documentary, *Wrestling*. See Scott MacKenzie, 'The Missing Mythology: Barthes in Québec', *Canadian Journal of Film Studies*, 6.2. (1998), pp. 65–74.

13   See Olivier Hadouchi, 'African Culture Will Be Revolutionary or Will Not Be': William Klein's Film of the First Pan-African Festival of Algiers (1969)', *Third Text*, 25.1 (2011), pp. 117–28.

14   Alison Smith, *French Cinema in the 1970s: The Echoes of May* (Manchester: Manchester University Press, 2005), p. 228. Some footage from *Maydays* also features in Marker's *Grin without a Cat/Le fond de l'air est rouge* (1977, Fr., 240 min.), as do shots from Raymond Depardon's *Ian Palach* (1969, 16 mm, col., 12 min.).

15   Michael Ryan, 'Militant Documentary: mai '68 par lui-même', *Ciné-Tracts*, 2.3–4 (1979), pp. 1–20.

5

One plus one (p.m.)

'68 helped ... to break the routine. (Jean-Luc Godard)[1]

Galvanised by China's Cultural Revolution, and liberation struggles in the Congo, Cuba, Vietnam, and elsewhere,
Jean-Luc Godard had been changing his film method and its
relations to politics since the mid 1960s. *La Chinoise* (1967,
93 min.) and *Week-end* (1967, 105 min.), for example, drew
directly from his recent associations with radical left-wing
groups – or *groupuscules*. In concluding *Week-end* with the end
title 'FIN DE CINÉMA' [sic], he even appeared to renounce
the entire ideological apparatus of cinema (including his own
former contributions to its operations), inaugurating instead
a new beginning for modes of film production and communication. Between December 1967 and January 1968, he filmed
Le Gai savoir/The Joy of Knowledge (1969, ORFT, 95 min.),
in which austere cinematographic staging is combined with
pop art, advertising, still photographs, animation, and comic
strip to accentuate the fraught dialectic between words and
images, rhetoric and truth. The following month, he was at
the vanguard of the demonstrations against the dismissal of
Henri Langlois from the Cinémathèque française; he then visited Cuba, and toured the US (speaking with students, and
joining the demonstrations at the trial of the Black Panther
activist, Huey P. Newton). In May, he accompanied the group
of French filmmakers who disrupted the – already floundering
– film festival at Cannes. These interventions paved the way
for the formation of the Dziga-Vertov Group (DVG), and in
the subsequent four years Godard devoted his talents to the
cause of revolutionary politics: dedicated to Maoism, the DVG

attacked capitalism and neo-imperialism, sovietism, and –
especially – revisionist left-wing intellectuals and trade union-
ists for their role in reproducing the very social elite that was
causing all the trouble in the first place.[2]

Godard's filmmaking at this time was also influenced by his
relationship with Anne Wiazemsky, who he met in 1966, and
married the following year, or as he nonchalantly recollected
in the 1980s: 'I fell in love with a student at Nanterre, so I
started going over there myself, and that's how *La Chinoise*
came to be.'[3] After working with Robert Bresson on *Au hasard,
Balthazar* (1965, b&w, 95 min.), Wiazemsky had decided to
complete her baccalaureate, and apply for a place on a degree
course. In autumn 1966, she was duly enrolled at the new –
and typically overcrowded – University of Paris campus in
Nanterre, an otherwise ramshackle and isolated district on the
outskirts of the capital. Although she would leave the university within a year, the circles in which she and Godard moved
during this period introduced them to an exciting community
of activist intellectuals, who – while affiliated to their own anarchist and *gauchiste* factions – were as one in their opposition to
the policies of the state and university authorities, policies that
were reducing their higher education to a pariah existence on a
segregated campus, a stone's throw from Nanterre's notorious
bidonvilles, or slums. In 1968 – with Wiazemsky at his side –
Godard was anticipating fundamental social change in France,
and soon found himself passionately involved in debating and
shaping that change.

Although his cinema has always been especially attentive
to politics, and its relations to art, Godard's work between
1968 and 1972 is sometimes regarded as rigidly doctrinaire,
and extreme in its application of Brechtian techniques to foreground his analysis of contemporary politics. Rarely screened
and for decades unavailable – even on VHS or DVD formats
– films such as *Wind from the East/Le Vent d'est* (1970, 16 mm,
100 min.), *Vladimir and Rosa/Vladimir et Rosa* (1971, 16 mm,
92 min.), or even, *Letter to Jane: An Investigation about a Still*
(Godard and Jean-Pierre Gorin, 1972, 16 mm, 52 min.), for
example, languished on the outskirts of Godard's *œuvre*, and

by the 1980s had acquired the status of arcane essay films, produced by diverse hands, and implicated in a bankrupt revolutionary project. While it is logical to confine the DVG to a history of the 1960s and early 1970s, and a history of that era's new culture of opposition to oppression, injustice, and excessive materialism, it is also worth considering how its version of Maoism was not incompatible with Godard's scepticism towards authorities and their institutions, and his essentially modernist preoccupation with how reality is constructed by these forces. Brechtian statements in his films at this time invariably articulate an artistic vision that enjoins the filmmaker to represent the particularity of the real through elliptical, ironic, and ambiguous associations (montage) rather than through the mirage of mimesis (realism). *Une femme est une femme* (Godard, 1961, 84 min.), for example, cites Brecht: 'Realism does not consist in reproducing reality, but in showing how things really are', and in 1970 – in a manifesto published in the inaugural issue of Peter Whitehead's *Afterimage* magazine – Brecht is again the vital touchstone: 'To say how things are real ... how things really are'.[4] Godard's cinema is never crudely propagandistic, and at any given time comprises its own array of aspirations, attachments, and contradictions – which is one reason why his work between the production of *Week-end* and the formation of the DVG cannot be regarded as transitional, in any perfunctory sense.

Throughout 1968, Godard continued making films that were as experimental in their reconfiguring of audiovisual and narrative forms as they were ambitious in the pursuit of a new audience: chiefly, *One Plus One* (1968, 100 min.), but also *Un Film comme les autres/A Film Just Like Any Other* (1968, 16 mm, 108 min.), his contributions to the *Ciné-tracts* project, and – finally – his failed collaboration with D. A. Pennebaker and Richard Leacock on *One A.M.* (*aka One American Movie*). When first released, *One Plus One* was hastily re-edited by its producers, who imposed an alternative ending, and preferred the title, *Sympathy for the Devil* (with a view to making the film a more lucrative production by emphasising the participation of the Rolling Stones). In its original form, however, the film provides important insights into the evolution of Godard's artistic methods, and his interest in where and how revolutionary politics intersects with popular culture. The *Ciné-tracts* project, on the other hand, reunited Godard with Chris Marker and Alain Resnais, and facilitated collaborations with filmmakers whose work would also become associated with political avant-garde groups from this era, such as: Philippe Garrel and Jackie Raynal (Zanzibar Films); Jean-Denis Bonan (Collectif Cinélutte), and Jacques Loiseleux (Groupe Medvedkine). It was demanding, agitprop filmmaking that made an impression on Godard's subsequent career, both as a member of the DVG, and beyond.

A single spark can start a prairie fire

There are no revolutionaries but the joyful, and no politically or aesthetically revolutionary painting without delight. (Michel Foucault)[5]

The May 1968 events in France briefly dissolved the distinction between artist and artisan, subordinating the canonical designation of (some) art to the demands of the popular moment. In the midst of mass demonstrations, strikes, and street violence, contemporary culture in Paris acquired a new edge, and an alternative politics of aesthetics. Art for ideology's sake became virtually axiomatic, as artists created graffiti, posters, satirical cartoons, screenprints, and photomontages in support of the revolutionary cause. The École nationale supérieure des Beaux-Arts was reincarnated as the Atelier Populaire (People's Workshop) by its staff and students; and for nearly two months it produced hundreds of political posters, many of them now as iconic as the early Soviet and Front Populaire art that inspired them. Meanwhile, on the other side of the Boulevard Saint-Germain, students and strikers – intellectuals and workers – occupied the Théâtre de l'Odéon, where they debated the condition of French theatre, culture, and – especially – the cinema. For many of those present, the cinema was a symbol of social and artistic freedom, and its assimilation into the mass communications ideological state apparatus – to borrow from the contemporary parlance – had to be resisted. During the Odéon debates, the establishment of a popular forum or États Généraux was first mooted as a replacement for the Centre National de la Cinématographie (CNC), the statutory body largely responsible for the film industry in France. The desire to liberate the cinema from state interference by abolishing the CNC and making production, distribution, exhibition (and admission) costs minimal – if not free to all – was both a product of the spirit of 1968, and an inadvertent consequence of the Langlois controversy, an incident that had further exposed the authoritarian mentality of the Fifth Republic.

Earlier in 1968, the decision by André Malraux's ministry of cultural affairs to engineer Henri Langlois' dismissal from the directorship of the Cinémathèque française had outraged filmmakers, audiences, and critics in France, and elsewhere. In the 1930s, Langlois had been one of the founders of the Cinémathèque, and in the years after the war he had become its mercurial patriarch, and an inspirational figure for many of the critics at *Cahiers du cinéma*, and those filmmakers associated with the French New Wave. His subsequent humiliation at the hands of the state provoked confrontations between protestors and the police. Eventually, Malraux reversed the decision of the Cinémathèque's executive committee, and Langlois was reinstated (albeit with a reduced budget and increased administrative responsibilities). However, the smouldering animosity left in wake of l'affaire Langlois reignited in May, and quickly spread to Cannes. It also raged on the rue de Vaugirard, where the inaugural meeting of the États Généraux du cinéma français took place on 17 May. By the end of the month the first issue of its magazine, *Le Cinéma s'insurge*, had been published, and a group of sympathetic filmmakers – including Godard, Resnais, Garrel, and Jean-Pierre Léaud – had responded to Chris Marker's suggestion that they collaborate on a series of short 16 mm film 'pamphlets' that could be screened (using a mobile projector) to groups of students, strikers, and other activists. Forty of these *ciné-tracts* were produced in May–June, each costing only 50 francs to make, and they remain a

tangible legacy of that États Généraux, exemplifying how the
work of film collectives from the late 1960s and early 1970s –
in France and beyond – could combine political commitment
with formal invention.

The *Ciné-tracts* project afforded Godard an opportunity to
make genuinely collaborative, political films designed to counter the version of events being depicted on the state-controlled
television news programmes, and the media more widely (and
Le Monde, in particular). Although most of the *ciné-tracts* (or
film-tracts) lasted only three minutes, there are clear similarities
with the collage techniques Godard had been developing in *Le
Gai savoir*, and his interest in the forms of graphic *détournement*
associated with letterism, and situationism: 'Predominantly
silent and shot in black and white, each work was made by
re-filming photographs of May 1968 and of current events in
the world, in order to create a brief visual collage [that] should
"contest-propose-shock-inform-question-assert-convince-
think-shout-laugh-denounce-cultivate" in order to "inspire
discussion and action".'[6] Although the *Ciné-tract* filmmakers
were committed to a policy of collective authorship, it is generally acknowledged that Godard completed between eight and
twelve individual films for the project, which are – according
to Sally Shafto – 'recognizable by his distinctive handwriting
over the still images'.[7] He also assisted in the photography and
editing of other *tracts*, including at least two with his friend,
the poet and art critic, Alain Jouffroy (who he had consulted
during the production of *La Chinoise*).[8] Not surprisingly, there
are formal similarities between the *ciné-tracts* and the films of
the DVG period (especially, *Letter to Jane*) but perhaps they
also deserve more attention in discussions of Godard's use of
superimposed or inscribed text (and images of text and photographs) and writing in his films and other artwork, more generally. The most successful *Ciné-tract* collaboration was between
Godard and the artist, Gérard Fromanger, and involved filming a painting rather than photographs: *Le rouge: film tract 1968*
(16 mm, 3 min.).

In 1965, under the presidency of Gilles Aillaud, and supported by other artists associated with the Narrative Figuration

movement, the Salon de la Jeune Peinture reasserted the radical credentials of contemporary art in France by banishing
abstract expressionist and pop artworks from its annual exhibition, on the grounds that – and contrary to popular opinion,
and the judges at the Venice Biennale – it was little more
than aesthetically banal and socially vacuous Americana.[9]
Narrative Figuration had emerged in the immediate aftermath
of the *Everyday Mythologies/Mythologies quotidiennes* exhibition the previous year, and was closely related to the New
Figuration style. However, Narrative Figuration encouraged
important variations on that style, variations motivated by its
more urgent social agenda as well as the desire to depict traces,
impressions, outlines of people – elements of figuration – and
their relationship to the commodities, and commercial world,
that surrounds them. By no means adverse to incorporating
images from popular culture, or resituating iconic images from
the history of art, into alternative contemporary contexts, the
adherents of Narrative Figuration often excelled in their use
of irony for satirical purposes. Fromanger became close to this
movement in 1965, and its distinctive colour formations and
visual wit was much in evidence during the events of May 1968
at the Atelier Populaire (Beaux-Arts), where he played a leading role in organising the design and printing of political posters. However, it was his paintings of 'bleeding' US and French
flags – the wounded republics – that caught Godard's eye.

Godard initially contacted Fromanger in June 1968, with a
view to learning how to draw and paint. They met in Godard's
duplex on rue Saint-Jacques and continued to meet regularly
– and collaborate – until Godard left for New York in the
autumn. According to Fromanger, no sooner had he demonstrated his 'bleeding' paint technique than Godard insisted
they should film it, and distribute it as a *film-tract*.[10] Perhaps,
Godard intended this as the final *tract* in the series, hence
its title. The resulting film is a fascinating combination of
documentary and animation in which the audience observes
red (paint) spread itself across – invade – the white and blue
panels of the French tricolour. The tendency within Narrative
Figuration to apply strong blocks of primary colours doubtless

appealed to Godard, whose preferred cinematographic colour palate shares that preference. As the red paint spreads across the surface of the tricolour, the film becomes an investigation into a series of conceptual relations: for example, that between stillness and movement, colour and space, composition and chance, stability and instability. Given its title and context, these relations immediately resonate with political significance, much more so than the ontological conundrum provoked by works such as Jasper Johns's *Flag* (1954), for example – although, not his later work, *Toxic Flag for the National Vietnam Moratorium* (1969). *Le rouge: film tract 1968* is a documentary on the making of an artwork, and a cinematic rumination on the meaning of colour, inscribing abstract forms with a history of contemporary political events. For Godard and Fromanger, the pre-eminent symbol of the French Republic in 1968 has become a 'Butcher's Apron', to borrow a popular anti-colonialist moniker for the British Union Jack.

On contradiction

> The Beatles and the Rolling Stones are very important because they are popular and intellectual at the same time. That is good. That is what I am trying to do in the movies. We have to fight the audience. (Jean-Luc Godard, February 1968)[11]

One Plus One originated in early spring 1968, after informal discussions between Godard and the producer, Eleni Collard.[12] The talent agent, Mim Scala, was instrumental in securing the involvement of the Rolling Stones, although 'Godard's original idea was to make a film about Trotsky, with John Lennon playing the part of the Russian revolutionary ... [however] Lennon proved extremely suspicious of Godard'.[13] Collard, meanwhile, secured financial backing for the project from Cupid Productions, a company recently formed by Michael Pearson and Iain Quarrier. London doubtless appealed to Godard: the city had re-emerged as a hub of political radicalism, with growing numbers of activists involved in organisations, such as Campaign for Nuclear Disarmament (CND),

Committee of 100, Racial Adjustment Action Society (RAAS),
Vietnam Solidarity Campaign, Women's Liberation, Institute
for Workers' Control (IWC), Agit-Prop Revolutionary Festival,
London Free School (LFS), *IT*, *Oz*, *Black Dwarf*, and various
other *succès de scandales*. Perhaps, Godard was also aware of the
Congress on the Dialectics of Liberation (and its offspring,
the Anti-University of London), which had been convened by
David Cooper and Joe Berke in July 1967.

The Congress drew together an array of radical artists,
activists, and New Left intellectuals, including Stokely
Carmichael (who had to be placated during one session by
Allen Ginsberg), Herbert Marcuse, R. D. Laing, C. L. R.
James, Carolee Schneemann, Michael X, John 'Tito' Gerassi
(Sartre's friend and authorised biographer), the ubiquitous
Julian Beck, and the American actor and founding member
of the Diggers, Emmett Grogan – who mischievously read out
translated passages from a speech by Hitler and passed it off as
his own work.[14] According to Tariq Ali, such was the impact
of Carmichael's speech that the United Coloured People's
Association promptly expelled all its white members, and
within a matter of months had reformed as the British Black
Panther movement.[15] Although Godard was in Switzerland
during the Congress, it is not far-fetched to suggest that some
of its high points – especially, Carmichael's performance and
Grogan's prank – found their way into *One Plus One*. Frankie
Dymon Jr. (aka Frankie Y), one of the principal Black Power
militants in film, was a close associate of Michael X (Abdul
Malik), the founding member of RAAS and leading light in
the LFS, who was controversially imprisoned in 1967 under the
British Race Relations Act for inciting violence against the
white population. Michael X enjoyed a certain notoriety and
celebrity status, and his trial and conviction was covered in
the British national press.[16] This aspect of London's political culture also resonated with Godard's direct experience
of the American Black Panthers: he had recently visited
Oakland, California, during the Newton trial, and he knew
the policies and various personalities associated with the
Party. Agnès Varda, for instance, had also just completed

Black Panthers (1968, 16 mm, 31 min.), a documentary made during a 'Free Huey' birthday rally held in February 1968, and which includes Carmichael's speech outside the Oakland Auditorium, as well as interviews with Kathleen Cleaver, and other women activists.[17]

One Plus One also offered Godard an opportunity to explore how the radical potential of the 1960s was being stylised, commoditised – undermined – by popular culture and the mass media. Like its cinematic relatives (for example, *Wonderwall* (Massot, 1968), *Performance* (Roeg and Cammell, 1970), *Leo the Last* (Boorman, 1970), *Joanna* (Sarne, 1968), and *Tonite Let's All Make Love in London* (Peter Whitehead, 1967)), the film belongs to the history of a particular London milieu of late 1960s – at the beginning of the end. The city had become synonymous with the fashion and celebrity culture of the 'swinging sixties', and despite Mick Jagger's participation in the anti-Vietnam demonstration that culminated in the 'Battle of Grosvenor Square' (in March 1968), his popular image was still that of the decadent dandy rather than the dissident visionary. The sequences in *One Plus One* featuring the Rolling Stones, for example, include figures such as Marianne Faithfull, Anita Pallenberg, Edward Fox, Michael Cooper (the photographer), and Christopher Gibbs (the antique dealer, designer, and trendsetter). Faithfull had previously featured in Godard's *Made in the USA* (1966, 85 min.), singing an a cappella version of 'As Tears Go By', and Fox's wife – the actress, Joanna David – has a small role in *One Plus One*. However, it would not be until the end of October 1968 that *Black Dwarf* would publish the lyrics to 'Street Fighting Man' and underwrite the subversive credentials of the Rolling Stones (at the expense of the Beatles).[18]

Within the context of Godard's artistic development, it is instructive to consider *One Plus One* in light of *Le Gai savoir*, a film that reveals much about how his film method was changing at this time, and why. In *Le Gai savoir*, for example, Godard adopts Jean-Jacques Rousseau's *Émile, or on Education/Émile, ou de l'éducation* (1762) to explore the possibility of 'a return to zero in cinematic form, a cancelling of all illusory modes, a movement to a knowing, imaginative inquiry that would do away with the old conventions'.[19] Banned when it was first published, Rousseau's *Émile* became a key work for the French revolutionary governments in the 1790s. Using the personae of two young protagonists (Émile and Sophie) to illustrate and debate his ideas, Rousseau's book outlined his influential theories of childhood, education, and citizenship. In Godard's film, these characters are renamed Patricia Lumumba (Juliette Bertho) and Émile Rousseau (Jean-Pierre Léaud), and the content of their discussions owes little to Rousseau's original novel-cum-treatise. What is significant is how the words, images, and soundtrack in *Le Gai savoir* interrogate and interrupt claims to absolute truth, transcendent values, authentic selfhood, and – most importantly of all – the transparency of language, especially the language of television and film, and the pseudo-democracy of the new mass media. In his influential 1975 essay, 'The Two Avant-Gardes', Peter Wollen commented that *Le Gai savoir* 'is not a film with a meaning, something to say about the world, nor is it a film "about" film ... but a film about the possibility of meaning itself, of generating new types of meaning.' In this regard, it also 'presents the language of Marxism itself, a deliberately chosen language, as itself problematic'.[20] Such concerns are also central to *One Plus One*, where Godard again parodies different documentary modes: for example, lampooning the interview or interrogatory techniques associated with television news and current affairs programmes, undercutting *cinéma vérité* with slapstick comedy during the *faux*-observational scenes when Wiazemsky's character furtively sprays graffiti in various locations, including a 'voice of god' narrator who reads from a spoof political–pornographic novel, etc. Interestingly, Godard took his title for *Le Gai savoir* not from Rousseau but from Nietzsche – whose 1882 book of that title comprises poems, songs, and prose ruminations on topics ranging from the art of the troubadour ('le gai savoir') to the death of God, and a theory of eternal recurrence.

Nietzsche and Rousseau were also profound influences on Jacques Derrida, especially in *Of grammatology/De la grammatologie* (1967), and he had described himself as being in his own student days 'the stage for the great argument between Nietzsche and Rousseau and I was the extra, ready to take on all the roles'.[21] In relation to the *mise en scène* of *Le Gai savoir*, Colin MacCabe even suggests the film is 'best understood in terms of revolutionary modernism': 'The cover of Derrida's 1967 classic *De la grammatologie* appears in the film, and while it would always be a mistake to assume that Godard had read a particular book, it is clear that *Le Gai savoir* is an attempt to deconstruct the conventional relations between sound and images.'[22] MacCabe also mentions Godard's sense of an affinity with Philippe Sollers, the novelist and founding co-editor of *Tel Quel*, who was exploring a theoretical rapprochement between Maoism and post-structuralism at the time of *La Chinoise*.[23] In one sense, it would be absurd to describe Godard's method as deconstructionist: he is a filmmaker not an academic philosopher, and in 1968 his work seemed increasingly aligned with a political ideology hardly in thrall to *différance*. However, as MacCabe's reference to Sollers implies, the dominant spirit and hermeneutic strategies of French philosophy in the 1960s inevitably made an impression on Godard. A critical activity – such as Deconstruction, for example – that demonstrates how the structures organising our perception of reality are entirely contingent on a system of oppositions that privilege one value system over the other, etc. is not incompatible with Godard's poetics of montage. It is inconceivable that Godard would not be sympathetic – if even, only in passing – to a critical attitude so determined to keep meaning perpetually in play by rigorously attacking the metaphysically fraudulent foundations of rational discourse: a world where the sum of one plus one never necessarily equals two is nothing if not amenable to the imagination of an artist like Godard.

One Plus One comprises ten sequences, five of which show the Rolling Stones at the Olympic Studios composing, rehearsing, and recording their song, 'Sympathy for the Devil'. Five 'acted' scenes alternate with these seemingly observational documentary sequences. Two of the staged scenes involve actors playing the role of Black Power militants based in a scrapyard beside Battersea Bridge Train Station; Godard's choice of this location – especially one full of wrecked and abandoned cars – calls to mind *Week-end*, and one of the title cards from its opening: 'Un Film Trouvé à La Ferraille' ('A Film Found in the Junkyard'). Two other sequences in *One Plus One* include a character, Eve Democracy (Wiazemsky): in one, she is being interviewed by a film crew in a wood or meadow; in the other she performs the role of a guerrilla or freedom fighter on a beach (in a film-within-the film sequence directed by a character played by Godard). Another of the staged sequences is set in a bookshop – selling pulp fiction, comics, political tracts, and pornographic magazines. The bookshop appears to be run by a man – dressed in a snazzy purple velvet suit – who constantly reads aloud passages from *Mein Kampf* (the role is performed by Quarrier), while the customers give Nazi salutes, and slap two hippies/students across the face before leaving. As mentioned above, *One Plus One* also includes short single-shot inter-scenes depicting a woman (Wiazemsky, again) spraying political graffiti on various objects and surfaces (a window in a Hilton hotel bedroom, a white wall, a red car, a blue yard door, and an advertising billboard, etc.).

Two other components of the film's *mise en scène* are noteworthy: the bright, colourful hand-painted inter-title cards (which – like the graffiti – play and pun on letters and parts of words), and the soundtrack (in which the diegetic dialogue and sound often compete – or overlap with – the 'narrator's' (Sean Lynch) readings from an absurd parody of a political–pornographic thriller, a fictitious fiction. The configuration of these parallel sounds – especially when they involve speech and music – not only detaches the image from the constraints of some otherwise facile narrative function, it also combines with Godard's extensive use of long, lateral tracking shots, and the film's vivid Eastmancolor palate, to defer closure, and resist a conventional means of articulating the meaning of the film – a vital aesthetic consideration completely lost on Quarrier (who was, after all, an actor and not a filmmaker) and Pearson when they changed the ending of the original film by including the band's full rendition of 'Sympathy for the Devil'. Under Godard's artistic direction, however, the film had emerged as a cinematographic exercise in keeping contradictions in play, not resolving them, or as Godard himself put it: '*One Plus One* does not mean "one plus one equals two".'[24] Unfortunately, the controversy that surrounded the premier of the producers' version has sometimes distracted from the complexity – and audacity – of Godard's vision of contemporary culture, and how the film indicts a certain form of radical politics as just another mode of popular performance. As the ethnomusicologist, Patrick Burke remarks: 'Rather than assume a direct, uncomplicated correspondence between the energy and style of rock and political and cultural revolution, Godard's film pushes viewers to acknowledge the then unfashionable possibility that both rock music and revolutionary politics are social and textual constructions created through the circulation of borrowed texts rather than rooted in any essential reality.' [25]

The documentary core running through *One Plus One* chronicles the Rolling Stones composing and recording 'Sympathy for the Devil', and their efforts to arrange its loose form into a viable track for their album, *Beggars Banquet*. At this stage, the song had the prosaic working title, 'The Devil Is My Name' (which is not very faithful to the ironic intricacies of the novel said to have inspired it, Mikhail Bulgakov's *The Master and Margarita* (1967)), but the work in progress invariably interests Godard more than the finished artefact. As the band discusses and rehearses parts of the song, the camera tracks around them – tracking the track, so to speak – stopping to frame someone playing, or waiting to be counted or cued in. It is tempting to speculate on how *One Plus One* notices Brian Jones's increasingly peripheral role in the band, and how it might even foreshadow his impending decline, and death. In reality, Jones seems no more excluded than Bill Wyman effetely shaking his maracas, or even Charlie Watts behind his drum kit, penned inside a makeshift sound-board capsule. What Godard's camera does capture in these moments is an impression that while the song remains uneven and unfinished, so too they – the band – do not exist collectively, and cannot perform as an artistic unit. As the music starts and stops, and people drift around the studio smoking, or technicians stand idly chatting,

10   *One Plus One*: Rolling Stones

the film evokes an atmosphere of sterility, and dead time, as well as one of frustrating collaborative labour.

Godard clearly identifies with these work-a-day artists, with a group of people – especially Keith Richards and Mick Jagger – who are trying to create something aesthetically meaningful. After all, there are obvious similarities between the recording studio and the film studio, and Godard is at ease in this milieu. On another level, the Rolling Stones also inhabit a problematic identity: they are, after all, a group of white middle-class Englishmen who make money appropriating and commercialising a musical style that belongs to black culture, i.e. by stealing from a history that has been violently oppressed by other white men. This contradiction is signified at the beginning of the first Black Power sequence in the film, when one of the militants (Limbert Spencer) sits in a wheelbarrow reading aloud a passage on the history of classical blues from LeRoi Jones's *Blues People: Negro Music in White America* (1963). The camera then tracks along a slow, circular path as it follows another character distributing rifles, while other black militants read from texts by iconic activists: Frankie Dymon Jr. (aka Frankie Y) reads aloud (and into a recording machine) from Stokely Carmichael's *Black Power: The Politics of Liberation* (1967), followed by another activist, reading from Eldridge Cleaver's autobiographical *Soul on Ice* (1968), in which the author is recounting his early experiences as a politically motivated rapist. At this point in the sequence, the action involves the agitprop abduction, torture and execution of three white women (blindfolded and wearing white night-dresses), and other militants (including Omar Diop) spraying graffiti (for example, 'FBI + CIA = TWA + PANAM'), and the names of murdered black leaders (such as Malcolm X, Patrice Lumumba, and Martin Luther King) on the scrapped cars piled around the yard.

In keeping with Godard's critique of the capitalist mass media – especially, its television news coverage – two sequences in *One Plus One* enact encounters between that media and a principal character: in 'All About Eve', Eve Democracy (Wiazemsky) is interviewed by a male reporter with a film crew; and in the other, 'Inside Black Syntax', a leader of the Black Power militants (Dymon Jr.) is interviewed by two young black women reporters (Glenna Forster-Jones and Monica Watters). In both sequences, the women characters are rendered powerless by the violence of rhetoric, regardless of whether they are interviewees or interviewers. Eve Democracy is bombarded with questions, many of which are just prefabricated slogans and aphorisms. She responds only with a 'Yes' or a 'No', and as the scene develops the interviewer's relentless diatribe about politics, culture, and drugs becomes increasingly abstract and absurd. (Apparently, Godard lifted many of the questions directly – if randomly – from a recent *Playboy* magazine interview with Norman Mailer.)[26] However, Godard's position is obvious enough: the media manufactures its own truth; there is never really an interview, only a dominant point of view being legitimised by the illusion of journalistic interaction, by a hermetically (and hermeneutically) sealed ideological apparatus. In other words, in the age of mass communications, the political interview is a performative rather than an interrogative act. The sequence is set in an idyllic woodland location – with exaggerated non-diegetic bird sounds added – and in Eve Democracy's hippie-like appearance and other-worldly demeanour, it accentuates the contradiction between a Rousseauist 'state of nature' and a capitalist culture awash with technologies of oppression masquerading as instruments of freedom (of speech). While Godard depicts Eve Democracy – or *naive democracy* – as a passive phenomenon constructed by the very authorities it claims to oppose, the Black Power movement is also depicted as problematic, and similarly susceptible to absurdity: Dymon Jr'.s rhetoric has to compete with loud shouting from other militants as they perform the business of revolution: guns, casualties, and destruction. In a film in which nothing is the sum of its parts, not even the Black Power movement is spared a confrontation with its own contradictions, contradictions that would ultimately weaken and divide the movement in the not-too-distant future. By 1970–71, for example, Newton and other Party members were increasingly disillusioned with its militaristic strategies, and frequent recourse to the rhetoric of violence, and – in a 1973 interview – Newton commented: 'I think rhetoric ran amok in the Black Panther Party while the leadership was under the influence of Eldridge Cleaver ... it caused murders of many of our people.'[27]

Despite the arithmetical connotations of its title, *One Plus One* is more concerned with literacy than numeracy: acts of writing and reading – rereadings – recur throughout the film and not solely in the sequences involving the militants. Take, for example, Quarrier's bookseller (reading from his copy of *Mein Kampf*), or Lynch's gravelly brogue as he voice-overs from the text of the spoof thriller – which creates another dimension to the soundtrack by overlaying and interrupting diegetic sound.[28] Even the Rolling Stones' recording session might be described as constituting a form of musical rewriting and political rereading. The literacy motif in *One Plus One* might also be derived from the strategies of *rereading* current within French intellectual life in the 1960s (and *La Chinoise*, again). For example, deconstructionist practices invariably subvert the relationship between reading and writing, wherein reading becomes the creative act, a form of writing, a rewriting – as demonstrated in Derrida's 'The Written Being/The Being Written' essay in *Of Grammatology*. Regardless of whether or not Godard immersed himself in specific texts and issues, the political hermeneutics of reading was a central issue for *Tel Quel* at this time, and the post-structuralist project, in general. Even in a (structuralist) text such as *Reading Capital/Lire le Capital* (1968), for example, Louis Althusser *et al.* argued for a new 'symptomatic' method of reading *Capital*, an approach that *reads* to reveal an alternative understanding of the epistemological importance of Marx's structural analysis of production. Already, in *La Chinoise* – and *Le Gai savoir* – Godard had 'put into play Althusser's project of knowing what "seeing, listening, speaking, reading" mean', and *One Plus One* also develops an – albeit looser – intertextual relationship with Althusser, and Mao.[29]

Perhaps, *One Plus One* also 'puts into play' this project by taking some of its inspiration from Mao's famous essay on contradiction, which (like the *Little Red Book* and his essay, 'On Practice') had become widely available in French translation by the mid 1960s – through China's Foreign Languages Press – and feature in *La Chinoise*. These texts attracted growing numbers of Marxists looking for an alternative to Soviet-style communism, and an alternative to the (sovietised) Parti communiste française (PCF), and the Confédération générale du travail (CGT), France's main trade union grouping, which – if anything – seemed to be busy shoring up the status quo. In 'On Contradiction', Mao identifies an array of *particular* historical contradictions, differentiating between their types to highlight the necessity of allowing these contradictions to be treated as *dominant* when the need arose, to ensure the universal advancement of communism.[30] While the myriad juxtapositions, ironies, and metaphors that feature in *One Plus One* are derived more from contemporary events (and Godard's evolving artistic style) than Maoist theory per se, there is – nevertheless – something about that theory – at the time, and

11   *One Plus One*: Black Power

in that place – that also coincides with Godard's film sense, and his characteristically sceptical view of whatever version of reality is being promoted by those with power and influence, including certain violent revolutionaries. There are no heroes in *One Plus One*, no rousing call to arms or revolutionary manifesto, only *particular* contradictions, and even these contradictions are open to contradiction: white musicians capitalising on black culture, black activists fetishising militarism, a mass media mystifying democracy, freedom of expression censoring expressions of freedom, and so forth.

The film's concluding sequence, 'Under the **Stones** the Beach', was shot on location, at a beach – quite possibly, in Weston-Super-Mare. The inter-title refers to one of the great slogans from the events of May '68: 'Sous les pavés, la plage!' (i.e. beneath the [regulated or chartered] cobble-stoned streets [of the capital], there is the beach [i.e. nature, freedom, eve(n) democracy]). The beach in *One Plus One*, however, is no windswept wilderness or coastline of unspoilt beauty but an

English holiday resort, strewn with deckchairs and decanted day trippers. In *At the Beach/Sur la plage* (1994), the anthropologist, Jean-Didier Urbain remarks: '[T]he myth of community haunts the seaside imaginary; it is not dismantled at the beach, [on the contrary,] the various segregations that sharply divide up the space splinter, scatter, and multiply its applications in the name of homogeneity.'[31] Urbain's touristic beach is a busy site of social and environmental contradiction, a frontline in the battle between identification and alienation, place and non-place, familiarity and modernity. In *One Plus One*, Godard similarly subordinates the recreational connotations of the seaside to confrontational ones, where even the cinema itself is thrust into the midst of a particular kind of battleground with iconic associations to newsreel images of the D-Day landings on the beaches of Normandy, and contemporary films of the Second World War, such as *Beach Red* (1967, Cornel Wilde, UA).

The sequence begins with Eve Democracy running into Godard's tracking shot, carrying a rifle and accompanied by an African revolutionary (presumably), who is also armed. Shots can be heard and other armed figures run across the beach, as she falls, and is then dragged back on to her feet by her comrade-in-arms. She runs across the camera tracks, past Godard, and towards the 'Mighty Sam' camera crane now dominating the foreground. Other shots ring out, and she falls again. Godard runs over, and pours some red paint on her white coat. Lynch's voice is heard clearly on the soundtrack: 'Now I was on the beach waiting for Uncle Mao's yellow submarine to come and get me.' Meanwhile, Eve Democracy is placed – lying on her side – on the chair of camera crane, between two flags, one red (communism), and the other black (anarchism). She is then lifted up into the sky, as the arm of the crane swoons and then rises into the sun.

Perhaps, this sequence is best considered in relation to Wiazemsky's earlier Eve Democracy incarnation in the film (in which she is bombarded with rhetorical slogans by the television interviewer/ee) rather than as a cryptic commentary on her relationship with Godard, and their differences of

opinion regarding the effectiveness of revolutionary struggle.
Now, on the beach rather than in the woodland, Eve/idealism
is playing the role of someone who has taken up arms, joined
forces with other liberation struggles, and become a martyr to
the cause. (There are also faint traces in this denouement of
Godard's original scenario for *One Plus One*: a tragi-comedy of
love about a young French woman living in London who falls
in love with a Black Power militant, who was to be played by
Michael X.) The machinery of cinema facilitates her apotheosis – with a camera crane – and as her body is lifted into the
skies, so too Godard confronts the audience with the film's
central question or problem: what if particular forms of radical
politics – Eve Democracy, or Black Power militancy, or both
– are simply new creations of a mass media, politically ineffec-
tual cultural fads – like the Rolling Stones – with nothing of
real significance to contribute to the change in consciousness
needed to change society?

Pay attention to methods of work

This is not the film Jean-Luc intended as *One American Movie*
(*1 AM*). Rather, he called it a parallel movie, *1 PM*. (*1 PM*, opening title card)[32]

Although Godard was impressed by Richard Leacock's and
D. A. Pennebaker's technological innovations, and had
employed Albert Maysles as principal cameraman on
Montparnasse et Levellois (1965, 16 mm, 18 min.), he had also
ridiculed the US 'direct cinema' style, and the fastidious
Leacock, in particular.[33] For Godard, any notion that reality could be rendered without acknowledging, incorporating,
interrogating the filmmaking process itself – the participation
of the camera – exemplified *naïveté* not *vérité*. Nevertheless, in
the autumn of 1968, he travelled to New York City to begin
making a film with Pennebaker and Leacock, provisionally
entitled *One A.M.* (*One American Movie*).

Disappointed by the experience of *One Plus One*, Godard
was also despondent as the much-vaulted sea change in France
began to resemble a freak wave: the Gaullists triumphed in

legislative elections at the end of June 1968, while the *les accords de Grenelle* had duly placated the rump of the trade union movement. Increasingly, he sensed the US offered more fertile terrain for revolutionary activism. By 1968, its youth culture had become more outspoken in its opposition to the powers-that-be, and recent events had further disturbed the status quo: the assassinations of Martin Luther King and Robert Kennedy; the Tet Offensive, and its paradigmatic impact on US public opinion of the Vietnam War; and the violence at the Democratic National Convention in Chicago. In his travels around the US in 1967–68, Godard had not only come into contact with groups such as the Civil Rights Movement and the Black Panther Party, he was also introduced to the mass demonstrations organised by the National Mobilisation Committee to End the War in Vietnam ('the Mobe'), Students for a Democratic Society (SDS), and the activities of the Youth International Party, or the Yippies, whose Provo-style happenings and 'pie-ing' antics (i.e. throwing custard pies at people) introduced a genuinely anarchic dimension to the US counter-cultural scene. Again, Godard wanted to capture on film – and participate in – the historic revolutionary convulsion he hoped was about to take place.

The film Godard originally planned resembles a companion piece to *One Plus One*, or – perhaps – a corrective to *Sympathy for the Devil*. It was to include ten sequences, five conventional documentary pieces that would alternate with five dramatised scenes. The documentary components would involve: interviews with a woman working on Wall Street; the political activist, Tom Hayden; Eldridge Cleaver; a girl from a poor neighbourhood in Brooklyn; and the Jefferson Airplane performing ('House at Pooncil Corners') on the roof of the Schuyler Hotel on 45th Street, in Manhattan. The staged scenes would comprise an actor reading the words (or lyrics) spoken (performed) in the previous documentary sequence. Godard would direct and edit *One AM*, while Pennebaker and Leacock would be responsible for its cinematography and sound. Rip Torn was hired as the principal actor in the film; he had recently worked with Pennebaker and Leacock on Norman Mailer's *Maidstone*

(1970, 16 mm, 110 min.) – and had also, coincidentally, played one of the leading roles in *Beach Red*. The association between *One A.M.* and Mailer is indirect but not insignificant. Mailer's *Armies of the Night: History as a Novel/The Novel as History* was published in early spring 1968, and rendered parallel accounts (one historical, the other fictional) of the Mobe's anti-Vietnam War March on the Pentagon the previous year (during which Mailer had been arrested). In the course of the novel, Mailer uses autobiography to collapse the parallel structure of the book from within, emphasising the unreliable, indeterminate nature of historical narrative.

As with *One Plus One*, Godard had envisaged that *One A.M.* would adopt an open, reflexive, entropic form involving the audience in processes of finding and losing themselves, questioning the validity of documentary images as actual, factual evidence, and becoming more sensitive to the ideological discourses that frame the documentary image, especially within America's reactionary mass media. Changes were soon made to the original plan: a young employee at the Chase Manhattan Bank (Carol Bellamy) replaced the 'Wall Street woman'; the 'girl from the Ocean-Hill-Brownsville district in Brooklyn' was replaced by a classroom full of mainly black children from the same district; and Godard added a sequence involving LeRoi Jones performing his poetry in Newark, NJ – which in 1967 had witnessed a week of race riots that resulted in twenty-six fatalities, and hundreds of injuries (and Jones's arrest, and controversial trial). Rip Torn was required to wear various costumes while reciting the words of the interviewees/protagonists, including a Native American outfit, a Civil War confederate officer's uniform, and a modern US military uniform. The displacement of spoken language in this way was reminiscent of both *Le Gai savoir* and *One Plus One*, drawing attention to its essentially rhetorical and contingent nature. Interestingly, Cleaver is particularly antagonistic and suspicious of Godard, even when the director earnestly agrees with him about how the mass media distorts the Panther message. Perhaps, the most notable sequence in the film, however, involved the Jefferson Airplane impromptu concert, or 'guerrilla gig'. This

12   *One P.M.*

live musical performance – displaced, incongruous, and ille-
gal – was brought to an abrupt end with the arrival of the
NYPD, who arrest various members of the band, and Torn ...
inevitably.

Ultimately, Godard (with Jean-Pierre Gorin) abandoned
the *One A.M.* project during post-production, and decided to
return to editing the rushes from *Le Gai savoir*. They argued
that political circumstances had now changed, and that
Pennebaker and Leacock had proved too resistant to an alternative filmmaking experience, too reluctant to discard techniques synonymous with their own 'direct documentary' style
(as in, for example, *Dont Look Back* (1967, 16 mm, b&w, 96
min.): editing would take an age to complete, and would yield
nothing of much cinematic interest. Pennebaker, for his part,
was left heavily in debt and – in order to fulfil his contract
with the producers at Public Broadcasting Laboratory (PBL)
– he edited the footage into *One P.M. (One Parallel Movie)*. It
is difficult to piece together Godard's original vision for *One*

A.M. from Pennebaker's film, which is not to say it is without archival value, especially in tracing Godard's ideas about political filmmaking at the end of a year that had initially seemed to promise so much. In this context, it is an important work in relation to understanding Godard's broader engagement with US politics during this period, and his sources for DVG films such as *Vladimir and Rosa* – which 're-creates' the 1969–70 trial of the Chicago Seven.

Serve the people

In a contemporary review of *One Plus One*, Peter Whitehead commented: 'In his pessimistic reduction of language to a series of fragments of meaningless despair, Godard has created a film whose very structure symbolises the dislocation of Being and Existence that threatens us all.'[34] There is plenty of humour in Godard too, and 'sceptical' is a much better word than 'pessimistic' but the gist of Whitehead's observation is undeniable: in the final analysis, the fundamental crisis at the heart of '1968' for many intellectuals proved more existential than social, a station along the way towards individual enlightenment rather than a catalyst for permanent revolution. For Godard and Gorin, the Dziga-Vertov Group might do something to rectify these mistakes and perhaps keep the revolution – and its art – political.

Notes

1 Qtd. in Colin MacCabe, *Godard: A Portrait of the Artist at Seventy* (London: Bloomsbury, 2003), p. 213.
2 See David Faroult's various contributions to *Jean-Luc Godard: Documents*, eds Nicole Brenez *et al.* (Paris: Centre Pompidou, 2006), especially his 'Never More Godard: Le Groupe Dziga Vertov, l'auteur et la signature', pp. 120–6.
3 Qtd. in Keith Reader's *The May 1968 Events in France: Reproductions and Interpretations* (London: Macmillan, 1993), p. 146.
4 Godard, Jean-Luc, 'What Is to Be Done?', *Afterimage*, 1. (1970), npg.

5   Michel Foucault, 'Photogenic Painting', in *Revisions 2: Photogenic Painting: Gérard Fromanger*, ed. Sarah Wilson (London: Black Dog, 1999), p. 77.

6   Nicole Brenez, 'Forms: 1960–2004: "For It Is the Critical Faculty that Invents Fresh Forms"', in *The French Cinema Book*, eds Michael Temple and Michael Witt (London: BFI, 2004), p. 234.

7   Sally Shafto, 'Filmography', in MacCabe, *Godard: A Portrait of the Artist at Seventy*, p. 353.

8   Richard Brody, *Everything Is Cinema*, pp. 305–6. In addition to writing a book on Fromanger in the early 1970s, Jouffroy has also written extensively on William Klein's photography.

9   The Salon de la Jeune Peinture was itself criticised by conceptual and 'anti-painting' figures like Daniel Buren, Oliver Mosset, Michel Parmentier, and Niele Toroni (known collectively as 'BMPT') who argued that its radicalism was superficial. See Sami Siegelbaum, 'The Riddle of May '68: Collectivity and Protest in the Salon de la Jeune Peinture', *Oxford Art Journal*, 35.1 (2012), pp. 53–73.

10 See Gérard Fromanger, '*Le Rouge (1968)*', *Rouge*, 1 (2003), http://rouge.com.au/1/rouge.html This translation is an abridged version of his 'Il faut créer un Vietnam dans chaque musée du monde', in *Jeune, dure et pure! Une histoire du cinéma d'avant-garde et expérimental en France*, eds Nicole Brenez and Christian Lebrat (Paris/Milan: Cinémathèque Française/Mazzotta, 2001), pp. 336–8.

11 Gene Youngblood, 'Jean-Luc Godard: No Difference between Life and Cinema [1968]', in *Jean-Luc Godard: Interviews*, ed. David Sterritt (Jackson, MS: University of Mississippi Press, 1998), p. 15.

12 Originally from Greece, Collard had produced a political allegory, *Vortex/To prosopo tis Medousas* (Nikos Koundouros, 1967, 90 min.) that had been banned by the Greek (military) government of the day. She then moved to London, was active in feminist circles (hence, her interest in Godard's work at that time), before becoming the co-founder of the Committee for the Reunification of the Elgin Marbles.

13 MacCabe, *Godard: A Portrait of the Artist*, p. 211. See also Mim Scala's *Diary of a Teddy Boy: A Memoir of the Long Sixties* (London: Creative Space, 2013), pp. 95–9. In one of the sequences from *British Sounds/See You at Mao* (1969, 16 mm, 52 min.), a group of

University of Essex students attempt to radicalise Beatles' songs (namely, 'Hello, Goodbye', and 'Revolution') by creating new political lyrics. At the end of 1968, the – supposedly, counter-revolutionary – lyrics of 'Revolution' had provoked a war of words between Lennon and the editors of *Black Dwarf*. See Tariq Ali's *Street Fighting Years: An Autobiography of the Sixties* (London: Verso, 2005), pp. 356–60.

14 See Brian Thill's 'Black Power and the New Left: The Dialectics of Liberation, 1967', *Mediations: Journal of the Marxist Literary Group*, 23.2 (2008), pp. 119–34.

15 Ali, *Street Fighting Years*, pp. 198–9.

16 In 1975, Michael X was convicted and hanged for his part in a double-murder in Trinidad, where he had set up an agricultural commune. One of the victims was Gale Benson, the daughter of Leonard Plugge, a flamboyant Conservative MP (whose house in Lowndes Square had been used as the principal set during the production of *Performance*). She had come to Trinidad with her then partner, Hakim Jamal, the Black Panther activist, who had achieved notoriety through his affair with Jean Seberg in the late 1960s. See John L. Williams's *Michael X: A Life in Black & White* (London: Random House, 2008); V. S. Naipaul's *The Return of Eva Perón, with The Killings in Trinidad* (New York: Knopf, 1980).

17 On 27 February 1968, Godard, Varda and Jacques Demy participated in a panel discussion at the University of Southern California (USC). See Youngblood, 'Jean-Luc Godard: No Difference between Life and Cinema', pp. 15–26.

18 Interestingly, the biographies of the various people associated with the making of *One Plus One* contribute generously to the complicated mythology of the 'swinging sixties'. Pearson, for example, was the son of a British aristocrat (Viscount Cowdray) who was reputed to be the second largest landowner in Sussex, while Quarrier was a self-taught actor and photographer from Canada, who was – in 1968 – living with the US model, Donyale Luna (who features in Klein's *Who Are You, Polly Maggoo?*) in a Chelsea apartment they co-owned with Roman Polanski and Sharon Tate. By the end of the 1970s, Brian Jones had drowned in his swimming pool; Sean Lynch – the narrator in the film – had been killed in a car accident (after spending a year in a Spanish prison for drug offences); Sharon Tate had been murdered by Charles Manson's 'Family'; Quarrier had been institutionalised after suffering a mental breakdown; and Donyale Luna – like

Michael Cooper – would fatally overdose on heroin. In May 1973, Omar Diop, who features in the film as one of the militants, died in Senegal's atrocious Goree Island prison (after being severely beaten, and then denied medical attention), while serving a three-year sentence for 'offenses against the state'. A contemporary of Wiazemsky at Nanterre, Diop had previously appeared in *La Chinoise* (as the Marxist student-lecturer, 'Comrade X'). See Anne Wiazemsky's *Une année studieuse* (Paris: Gallimard, 2012), pp. 157–80. In *La Chinoise*, perhaps, the name 'Comrade X' not only refers to Malcolm X, but also to King Vidor's romantic comedy (set in the USSR), *Comrade X* (1940, MGM).

19   Robert Philip Kolker and Madeleine Cottenet-Hage, 'Godard's *Le Gai savoir*: A Filmic Rousseau?', *Eighteenth Century Life*, 11 (1987), pp. 118–19.

20   Peter Wollen, *Readings and Writings: Semiotic Counter-Strategies* (London: Verso, 1982), pp. 100–1.

21   Jacques Derrida, 'A "Madness" Must Watch Over Thinking', in *Points … Interviews, 1974–1994*, ed. Elisabeth Weber (Stanford, CA: Stanford University Press, 1995), p. 324.

22   MacCabe, *Godard: A Portrait of the Artist*, p. 207.

23   *Tel Quel* did not reciprocate Godard's enthusiasm for their work. Marcelin Pleynet, for example, dismissed *La Chinoise* and Godard's political aesthetic. See 'Economic–Ideological–Formal: Interview with Marcelin Peynet [1969]', trans. Elias Noujaim, in Sylvia Harvey, *May '68 and Film Culture* (London: BFI, 1978), pp. 149–64.

24   Richard Roud, *Jean-Luc Godard* (London: BFI/Thames & Hudson, 1970), p. 150.

25   Patrick Burke, 'Rock, Race, and Radicalism in the 1960s: The Rolling Stones, Black Power, and Godard's *One Plus One*', *Journal of Musicological Research*, 29:4 (2010), p. 277 (pp. 275–94).

26   Richard Brody, *Everything Is Cinema: The Working Life of Jean-Luc Godard* (New York: Henry Holt, 2008), p. 340.

27   Qtd. in Howard Caygill, 'Philosophy and the Black Panthers', *Radical Philosophy*, 179 (2013), p. 11.

28   For more detailed discussion on the bookshop/'Heart of the Occident' sequence in *One Plus One*, see Kevin J. Hayes's 'The Book Motif in *One Plus One*', *Studies in French Cinema*, 4.3 (2004), pp. 219–28.

29   Jacques Rancière, *Film Fables*, trans. Emiliano Battista (Oxford: Berg, 2006), p. 144.

30   See Slavoj Žižek, 'Mao Zedong: The Marxist Lord of Misrule',
      in *On Practice and Contradiction*, Mao-Tse-Tung (London: Verso,
      2007), pp. 1–28.
31   Jean-Didier Urbain, *At the Beach*, trans. Catherine Porter
      (Minneapolis, MN: University of Minnesota Press, 2003), p. 205.
32   *1 P.M. (One Parallel Movie)* (Pennebaker, 1972, 16 mm, 95 min.).
33   See Keith Beattie, *D. A. Pennebaker* (Champaign, IL: University
      of Illinois Press, 2011), pp. 68–73. In addition to a series of with-
      ering comments on Leacock in a 1964 *Cahiers du cinéma* survey
      of US directors, Godard had also cast Jean Seberg as 'Patricia
      Leacock' – a hapless *Reader's Digest* correspondent – in his short
      film, *The Big Swindler/Le Grand Escroc* (1963, 20 min.).
34   Whitehead, 'One Plus One [1968]', *Framework*, 52.1 (2011),
      p. 395. Coincidentally, Whitehead had made the Rolling Stones's
      first documentary three years earlier: *The Rolling Stones: Charlie
      Is My Darling: Ireland, 1965* (1965, b&w, 64 min.); Nicole Brenez,
      '"The Ultimate Doomed Victims of the Romantic Dream": Jean-
      Luc Godard/Peter Whitehead', *Framework*, 52.1 (2011), pp. 367–
      85. On *Charlie is My Darling*, see Michael Chanan's 'Shooting
      Star: Peter Whitehead and the 1960s Documentary', *Framework*,
      52.1 (2011), pp. 326–31.

6

Journey to Central Park

There are roughly three New Yorks. There is, first, the New York of the man or woman who was born there, who takes the city for granted and accepts its size and its turbulence as natural and inevitable. Second, there is the New York of the commuter – the city that is devoured by locusts each day and spent out each night. Third, there is the New York of the person who was born of somewhere else and came to New York in quest of something. Of these three trembling cities, the greatest is the last – the city of final destination, the city that is a goal. (E. B. White, *Here Is New York* (1948))[1]

By the end of 1980, New York was careering into another fiscal crisis. Its brush with bankruptcy in 1975–76 – and the ensuing chaos that culminated in the infamous blackout of July 1977 – was still fresh in the civic memory.[2] Demographic habits had continued to exacerbate racial polarisation, and the 'dual city' metaphor had by now become a journalistic cliché. Urban policy continued to be perilously ad hoc and indifferent to minority interests – despite the fact that (according to the 1980 census) New York had become a 'majority minority city' with 45 per cent of its population born outside the US (or in Puerto Rico), and with Hispanic and black immigrants still heavily concentrated in the lowest paid jobs. In 1980, New York recorded the highest number of street robberies of the ten largest cities in the US, and approximately 1,670 murders occurred that year: the highest on record, and only to be surpassed at the height of the Crack Wars of the late 1980s and early 1990s. A twelve-day subway strike in early spring had exposed its dangerous, dilapidated public transport system, and the inadequate resolution of this dispute would damage industrial relations between the city and its service sector for over a decade.[3]

Meanwhile, in the midst of a national recession and rising inflation, Ronald Reagan was being sworn in as the country's fortieth president, and Christmas Day would mark the first anniversary of the Soviet occupation of Afghanistan. The deaths that year of figures such as Jean-Paul Sartre, Roland Barthes, Alioune Diop, Henry Miller, Dorothy Day, and Marshall McLuhan (not to mention the complicated downfall of Louis Althusser) also conspired to associate 1980 with the end of a progressive attitude that had defined the 1960s. Yet, perhaps nothing symbolised the dissolution of an epoch, and the decline of the once great city, as poignantly as the killing of John Lennon. Commenting in *Punch* a week or so after the event, George Melly reflected: 'The sheer bulk of [Lennon's] obituaries is mysterious, beyond logic. Nothing he hoped for came about: wars rage, people hate, a young man buys a gun and waits outside the Dakota building; and yet everyone, it seems, feels diminished by his death.'[4]

Shortly after he had been shot by Mark Chapman, Lennon was rushed to a nearby hospital, and pronounced dead shortly afterwards. Yoko Ono was then taken back to their apartments in the Dakota to inform family and close friends. Outside, a large crowd had gathered to light candles, place makeshift wreathes, sing and play music. In the early hours of the morning, Ono sent a message to the mourners, asking them to disperse, and requesting instead that they gather 'anywhere and everywhere' for 'ten minutes of silent prayer' the following Sunday, at 2.00 p.m. Later that day, Ed Koch, the city's maverick Democrat Mayor, officially invited people to gather in Central Park for the vigil. Approximately 250,000 people attended, spreading across the park, along the Mall, and towards the police barriers and funereal flotsam now surrounding the front of the Dakota. While the cultural trauma of Lennon's death was amplified by an instant whirl of media interest, and similar vigils held in other cities around the world, the Central Park event was especially poignant, and symptomatic of how the killing of Lennon caught the conscience of advanced western societies generally too busy for death, and the work of mourning.[5] Perhaps, the grief of those who gathered in the Park that chilly Sunday afternoon (mainly white, middle class, and not quite middle-aged) had more to do with the phenomenon of symbolic loss and generalised social anxiety than the sudden death of the man who had given the world songs like 'Imagine'. After all, Chapman's act also further undermined the crumbling mythology of New York City, a place Lennon himself – paraphrasing a previous *poète maudit* – had once fondly likened to 'a little Welsh village with Jones the Fish and Jones the Milk, and where everybody seems to know everybody'.[6]

Fluxus and the walrus

> SCOTT MACDONALD: The last reel [of *Lost, Lost, Lost* (1976)] has the John Lennon/Yoko Ono passage. Did you know them?
>
> JONAS MEKAS: Yes, I knew Lennon. I'd known Yoko since 1959 or 1960 perhaps. Around 1962 she left for Japan and then decided to come back to New York. But she needed a job, for immigration, so *Film Culture* gave her first official job in this country. We have been friends ever since.[7]

For over six decades, Jonas Mekas has been creating a cinematic almanac of everyday events that he assembles into portraits, elegies, and sketches. In compilation works such as *Walden (Diaries, Notes, and Sketches)* (1969, 180 min.), *Lost, Lost, Lost* (1976, 178 min.), and *Paradise Not Yet Lost/Oona's Third Year* (1979, 98 min.) excerpts and fragments from Mekas's footage are edited into loose segments, usually captioned by typed and handwritten (often ironic) inter-titles. The films make use of natural ambient noise and (background) music, and can include Mekas's own tentative commentaries. Words such as 'notes', 'scenes', 'excerpts', 'sketches' (like the word 'lost') recur throughout his film *œuvre*, and writings. Despite its haphazard appearance, however, his technique adheres to a discernible aesthetic of informality, interruption, and fragmentariness that combines hand-held single frame shooting with random exposures, superimpositions, and varied projection speeds.

This practice gives the images an impressionistic flutter-effect, an effect synonymous with the Bolex, and also associated with the (albeit more austere) 'flicker' film techniques developed in the 1960s by people like Paul Sharits, Peter Kubelka, and Stan Brakhage.

Mekas, meanwhile, would resist notions of a personal style or discernible aesthetic. He does not necessarily see himself as a filmmaker, as one who directs – *makes* – films in any conventional or auteurist sense, even an artist-filmmaker sense. Instead, he prefers terms such as 'filmer', i.e. one who merely points his camera at whatever is there, whenever he has the inclination to do so, and then selects shots and sequences for occasional works. When footage is reassembled for an alternative film, it is done more in the spirit of a creative archivist than a dutiful chronicler of people and places past.[8] And yet, for all their artful incoherence, the works also have a distinctively wistful quality to them, as if holding out against abstraction, insisting on significance in the midst of their own loose, unsteady, fragile forms. *Scenes from the Life of Andy Warhol* (1990, 36 min.), *Zefiro Torna, or Scenes from the Life of George Maciunas* (1992, 34 min.), and *He Stands in a Desert Counting the Seconds of His Life* (1985, 149 min.), for example, are simultaneously personal *and* public elegies to artists and friends. To paraphrase Maureen Turim (writing on the paradoxes that complicate so-called 'autobiographical film-making' techniques in *Reminiscences of a Journey to Lithuania* (1972, 88 min.)), Mekas's films 'suggest in their gaps and processes a poetics of our displaced and conflicted selves; at their best, they express more than they know'.[9] In taking his camera for a walk in this way, Mekas has succeeded in creating an expansive body of cinematic work that criss-crosses between documentary forms and avant-garde praxis, history and memory, life and art.

Born in 1922, not far from the Lithuanian city of Biržai, Mekas arrived in New York City with his brother, Adolphas, in 1949. In the closing stages of the Second World War, he had been sent by the Nazis to a Forced Labour Camp near Hamburg, and after the war he spend time working and studying in West Germany before being resettled in the US as part of the Displaced Persons Program. Moving into the Williamsburg neighbourhood in Brooklyn, the brothers soon made friends with other Brooklyn-based artists and intellectuals, many of who were also recent refugees from post-war Europe. The diary films began in the early 1950s as a pastime that accidentally acquired larger expressive and historical significance. Paradoxically, it is largely because of their incidental style, their apparent tendency towards spontaneity, snapshot improvisation, and flicker-montage techniques, that they can constitute such a distinctive record of New York's post-war film and wider artistic culture. Mekas's creative, critical, and curatorial activities throughout this period have ranged from filming theatrical dramas (most notably, the Living Theatre's production of *The Brig* (1964, 65 min.)) to multimedia installations, poetry, criticism, and publishing; he was a founding editor of *Film Culture* in 1954, and for many years a film critic for *The Village Voice*. He initiated and participated in numerous avant-garde projects, political protests, and cultural collaborations (not least of which being the Filmmakers' Cooperative, and the Filmmakers' Cinémathèque/Anthology Film Archives project).

One of his closest artistic associations throughout the 1960s and 1970s was with the Fluxus group, and in particular with its original leading light (and a fellow Lithuanian émigré), George Maciunas (1931–78). Although never a fully-fledged Fluxus artist per se, Mekas's cinematic method has clearly been influenced by that environment. Like Pop, Minimalism, and New Realism, Fluxus was – and still is – dedicated to eradicating distinctions between elite and popular culture, between the subject of art and the object of life. However, it is also much more committed than most modern art movements to being a mode of action, a direct assault on the notion of art as art, on its academic categories and disciplines, and – faithful to its Dadaist forebears, and Provo neighbours – it has remained resolute in its belief that the sooner the institutions and aura of art become redundant, the better, or, as Arthur Danto explains:

> The revelation of Fluxus was that everything is marvellous. One did not especially need to single out soup cans or comic strips like Pop, industrial products like Minimalism, underwear and automobile tyres like the New Realists. Art was not a special precinct of the real but a way of experiencing whatever – rainfall, the babble of a crow, a sneeze, a flight of a butterfly, to list some of Maciunas's examples.[10]

Anti-object and interactive, conceptual and instructional, anonymous, undisciplined, polemical, playful, and the original source of 'happenings' and mail art, the spirit of Fluxus continues to provoke the world of contemporary art and conceptualism to a surprising extent – although, it is important to distinguish between European, North American, Japanese, and other varieties of Fluxus, and to avoid over-emphasising the importance of Maciunas (particularly, if at the expense of a more recent history of Fluxus).[11] While it is inadvisable to generalise about its place within some wider avant-garde culture, it would be true to say that the experiential, pedagogical, and intermedial strategies of Fluxus sought to subvert such intellectual categories while simultaneously depending on them for its identity. As Danto also points out, there are interesting affinities between Fluxus and Joseph Cornell:

> There is an ingratiating lightness to Fluxus art, even a certain playful innocence. In part this is because so much of it consists of playthings – cheap objects from the five-and-ten, like the balls and marbles Joseph Cornell vested with such magic when he juxtaposed them in boxes behind glass. Indeed, exactly the things that turn up in Cornell's boxes, including vintage engravings, are to be encountered in Fluxus objects ... But none of it is really intended to induce the sense of uncanniness and beauty one feels in the presence of Cornell's work.[12]

Caveats and comparisons aside, throughout the 1960s and 1970s Fluxus, with the mercurial Maciunas at the helm, was a genuinely influential artistic movement, and its impact was keenly felt in the world of experimental filmmaking at this time, especially in New York City.

In 1965, for example, Maciunas and Mekas devised the Fluxfilm Anthology to produce and exhibit short experimental films by artists currently associated with Fluxus. By 1970, the Anthology has gathered over forty works, many of which responded ingeniously to Maciunas' ludic manifesto. Some were conceived as elements in a larger intermedial event, others devised to be screened in a continuous loop, and only a few films seemed to fall foul of the lyrical seriousness sometimes associated with avant-garde film culture in New York at this time. The Fluxfilms play with simple, reductive, elementary – if now familiar – notions: the smile, a gesture, numbers, measurements, dates, words, fixed spaces. Maciunas' *10 Feet* (1966, 12.4 sec.), for example, consists of nothing other than ten feet of clear film leader, numbered one to ten. George Brecht's *Entrance to Exit* (1966, 6.30 min.) plays with concepts of entering, egress, arrival and departure, before fading to black, while *Trace #22* (Robert Watts, 1966, 1.15 min.) is a silent X-ray sequence of a mouth eating and speaking, and musician John Cale's *Police Car* (1966, 1 min.), simply the blinking lights of a police car. The Anthology films by Yoko Ono are especially notable examples of the Fluxfilm vision: *Eyeblink* (1966, 1 min.) is a slow-motion view of an eye blinking; *One* (1966, 4.30 min.) is a close-up of a striking and exploding match; while *Four* (1966, 5.30 min.) – anticipating her later *No. 4 (Bottoms)* (1966, 80 min.) and *Up Your Legs Forever* (1970, 70 min.) – is a witty study of human buttocks and their movements.[13] Although Ono's name first became associated with Fluxus around the time of her controversial performances of *Cut Piece* (1964), she never wanted to be part of its inner circle, as Danto comments in his catalogue essay for a retrospective of her work in 2000: 'Ono's relationship to Fluxus is a matter of delicate art-historical analysis, but if she fits in anywhere, it would have been in the world Maciunas created around himself, where the artist and their audience consisted of more or less the same people … a fragile underworld, easy not to know about [and] Ono's work from that era has the weight of winks and whispers.'[14]

The spirit of Fluxfilm would continue to influence Ono's later filmmaking projects, such as *Smile/Film No. 5* (1968, 58 min.) and *Fly* (1970, 19 min.), but as her relationship with

13   'John Lennon and Yoko Ono (Leaving Amsterdam, 31 March
     1969)'.

Lennon developed so too her filmmaking increasingly became
a vehicle for their musical collaborations. 'Two Minutes
Silence', from their 1969 album, *Unfinished Music No. 2: Life
with Lions*, for example, commemorates Ono's miscarried child
by paying homage to Cage's 1952 'proto-fluxus' composition,
4'33"; 'Listen, the Snow Is Falling', the B-side to their 1971
'Happy Xmas (War Is Over)' hit single, was inspired by Dick
Higgins's *Winter Carol* (1959); and a track on the *Mind Games*
album (1973), 'Nutopian International Anthem (3 Seconds of
Silence)', is indebted to Cage again, and to Maciunas' notion of
a conceptual republic of Fluxus, subsequently named 'Nutopia'
by Ono and Lennon. Fluxus was also important in their wider
attempts to 'overcome the contradictions between pop [music]
and avant-garde, to challenge bourgeois hegemony over the
pop audience', and although Ono was already an established
avant-garde artist (and composer) when she first met Lennon
in 1968, he – for all his hitherto erratic political behaviour –
sharpened the social focus of Fluxus (until the Nixon adminis-
tration began trying to deport him in 1972).[15]

Three friends

> Light a match and watch till it goes out. (Yoko Ono, 'Lighting
> Piece' (1957))

Mekas was naturally drawn into the whirlpool of artistic and
political activity generated by Maciunas and his friends but his
involvement was by no means uncritical and *Happy Birthday to
John* catches something of the complicated nature of Ono and
Lennon's relations to Fluxus, and the issue of their fame. The
film has a discernible dialectical structure, and comprises footage of Lennon and Ono at various events in the early 1970s (the
period between the release of *Let It Be* and his eighteen-month
'lost weekend'), before concluding with a montage of images
from Mekas's attendance at the Central Park vigil, along with
his wife (Hollis Melton), and their young daughter (Oona
Mekas). Although divided into six inter-titled segments, the
film initially seems to derive a clear two-part structure from its
soundtrack: the first placing Lennon's life at this time within
a convivial, carefree frame, accompanied by sounds of singing, banter, friends and possibilities, while the second deploys
sombre percussion music by Lithuanian avant-garde composer
Dalius Naujokaitis to enunciate a sense of foreboding. Despite
the convenience of this caesura, however, the film's structure
falls into three parts that can be delineated – notionally – as follows: first, 'Fluxus and Other Friends'; second, 'In Concert';
and finally; 'Vigil in the Park'. In fact, it is this trilogic structure that enables the film to avoid sentimental hagiography,
allowing space for a more sceptical perspective on the problematic relations between conceptual artists and dominant culture,
political activism and pop stars, communities and commodities, hypocrites and chequebooks. *Happy Birthday to John* is
nothing if not a moral tale.

The film begins with a sequence from the opening of Ono's
'There Is Not Here' exhibition at the Everson Museum in
Syracuse, New York, on 9 October 1971, the date of Lennon's
thirty-first birthday.[16] The soundtrack for the initial two minutes is taken from a recorded conversation between Lennon

and Mekas on the joys of Super-8 filmmaking, dated 19 December 1970. This is then replaced by ambient, unsynchronised noise and chatter from the exhibition press conference where Maciunas is seen (but not heard) addressing the assembled gathering of friends, journalists, and celebrities. Someone calls for the 'cameraman', while another starts chanting 'He's Got the Whole World', as Lennon is then framed fidgeting with a mirror cube. This moment is typical of how Mekas's sound–image manipulations and Bolex superimpositions appear to inadvertently generate motifs and extended metaphorical associations. Mirrors and reflections recur throughout the film (the ornate convex wall mirror in the hotel room, Ono's pilot sunglasses, the mirror lighting at the Madison Square Garden concert, etc.), as do shots of people using cameras, wearing glasses, looking to and away, and being on the edge or in a corner of Mekas's frame. Similarly, the refusal to synchronise sounds and images is always a strategy that will – despite itself – find alternative expressive possibilities ('at their best, they express more than they know'). The singing of 'He's Got the Whole World', for example, belongs to the post-exhibition birthday party held for Lennon in a room at the Hotel Syracuse. Phil Spector can be seen conducting the celebrity revellers, frantically strumming a guitar. Also in attendance at the party are people like Ringo Starr, Allen Ginsberg, Coby Batty (the Fugs), Klaus Voorman (Plastic Ono Band), Phil Oaks (producer), and the exhibition curators, David Ross and Jim Harithan. At one point, we see Lennon with his back to the camera, squatting on the floor, playing a guitar, and singing an impromptu version of 'Attica State', the protest song that would subsequently feature on *Some Time in New York City*, the commercially unsuccessful political album Ono and Lennon were working on at the time.[17]

The singing of 'Attica State' carries into the succeeding segments: brief out-takes from *Up Your Legs Forever* followed by footage from a party at producer Allen Klein's Riverdale home. Again, numerous stars and celebrities can be seen mingling and fooling around: Jerry Rubin, Ornette Coleman, Al Aronowitz; Andy Warhol taking photographs with his Polaroid 'Big Shot'

instant camera, Shirley Clarke being filmed filming (material
that would coincidentally feature in 'Part 1' of her experimental short, *The TeePee Video Spaces Troupe: The First Years, 1970–
1973*), Lennon playing basketball with Miles Davis, and both
admiring Lennon's psychedelic Platinum V Rolls-Royce, Ono
talking to Betty Mabry, and Lennon cheerfully sharing a joint
under a garden parasol as rain begins to fall. This shot marks
the first change in the film's mood and tempo; after it and
a few moments' silence, Naujokaitis' heavy percussion music
dramatically slows the film down even as rapid motion images
flutter past from Lennon and Ono's last headline performance
at a Madison Square Garden benefit concert (30 August 1972)
with Sha Na Na, Stevie Wonder, and Roberta Flack. The
segment ends with shots of the appreciative audience, before
finally cutting to an inter-title and the footage from Central
Park where another audience is now shown congregating for
the vigil.

Central Park has always been something of *locus amoenus* for
Mekas, most significantly in *Walden* where his vision of it as
a Thoreauian retreat from the busy metropolis, an innocent
space associated with wandering, picnics, and children playing
in the snow contrasts with Rudy Burckhardt's ominous short
documentary, *Central Park in the Dark* (1985, 7 min.), for example, or the tableau of observations in Frederick Wiseman's
Central Park (1990, 175 min.).[18] Mekas's romantic image of the
park remains largely intact in *Happy Birthday to John*, a film
that is both an ambivalent elegy for Lennon and a celebration
of the park as a vital, unifying civic space. It is also a home
from home for the immigrant, his reimagined Lithuanian
countryside in the middle of Manhattan. If anything, the film
associates the park with possibilities of freedom, peace, and
love. Alternating between shots of people moving, gathering,
and sitting in trees are shots of Mekas's daughter playing in
the leaves, a friend waving and smiling to the camera, a 'Peace
and Love' banner carelessly hanging from a park fence, and a
couple holding hands. In shots reminiscent of Cornell's *The
Aviary*, the film ends with the camera now pointed up into
the trees and towards the sky, before cutting to the child run-

ning through a pile of leaves, followed by three separate end-title cards, and a coda-image of a watercolour painting of wild strawberries.

Ten minutes

> I arrived in New York in the winter of 1980 with a friend. She had just found a job there, and we decided to share a studio. She would leave at dawn and not return until late in the evening. I hardly knew anybody, so I found myself walking all day long, wandering the city from top to bottom. (Raymond Depardon)[19]

By the end of the 1970s, Depardon had grown disillusioned with contemporary European photojournalism. The halcyon days of the international press pack and the post-war paparazzi were fading fast amid the exigencies of television news culture, the steady demise of quality magazines, and the pervasiveness of the 'decisive moment' photographic style. For Depardon, if being factual, objective – a reporter – meant producing formulaic images of spontaneous events, then he resolved to make his photography available to more impressionistic, unpredictable, and autobiographical qualities. He had become increasingly drawn to the expressionist and aleatory techniques of people like Robert Frank and William Klein, photographer-filmmakers whose images of New York, and the lives of its inhabitants in the 1950s, were again becoming influential. This transformation was not primarily about making photography and documentary film *artistic*, or making it more responsive to an aesthetic – rather than a journalistic – impulse, it was about allowing the images a meaning beyond the extreme transience of current affairs.

Depardon had been a successful photojournalist both within and beyond France: his work had garnered prestigious awards; he had co-founded the Gamma agency, and worked for other organisations including Dalmas and Magnum; he had travelled the planet and photographed some of the horrific consequences of war, famine, and poverty, as well as sublime landscapes, and bright, busy cities. In particular, he had worked extensively – and courageously – in Algeria, Vietnam, Chile, Biafra (Nigeria),

Lebanon, and Chad. In 1970, his business partner and friend, the photographer, Gilles Caron, was kidnapped, and then killed. In 1977, his interviews with François Claustre, a development worker held hostage by Hissène Habré's Chadian guerrillas, played a vital role in her subsequent release, and earned him a Pulitzer Prize. In 1979, after another exhausting assignment (this time in Soviet-occupied Afghanistan with Mujahedeen leader, Ahmad Shah Massoud, and some of his followers) he published his seventh book, *Notes*.[20] It comprises one hundred images, each accompanied by a caption that reflects on an elsewhere to the photograph, a caption that acts as a 'relay rather than an anchor', as he puts it.[21] *Notes* departs from conventional European photojournalistic practice and constitutes Depardon's first unequivocal attempt to replace an objective presentation of photographic 'evidence' with a subjective juxtaposition of image and text. Two other projects from this period are also related to his profound change in approach: the production of a second feature-length film, *San Clemente* (1980, b&w, 90 min.), and the photographs he took in New York City during 1980–81.

In *San Clemente*, the camera observes the lives of mentally ill patients, and their carers, in various Italian psychiatric hospitals, particularly one situated on the Venetian island of San Clemente. 'I felt at home there', Depardon later recalled, 'I was gaining precious knowledge of the art of photographing others without intruding on them – a necessary condition for anyone wandering those corridors and enclosed courtyards.'[22] The images of bewilderment in the film – the vacant and hidden looks, mannerisms, shuffles and utterances of its patients – are of course similar to other images and experiences from places of conflict and famine. The reticent framing of remoteness, desolation, and confinement has become a characteristic feature of Depardon's style: 'I don't like extracting lessons from things. I don't like giving lessons either.'[23] *San Clemente* also marks the beginning of his series of documentary films exploring the forms and effects of judico-legal, medical, and mass-media processes, films that observe people experiencing first-hand the panoptical capabilities of these systems, for example: *Caught in the Act/Délits flagrants* (1994, 109 min.), *Faits divers* (1984, 108 min.), *10th District: Moments of Trial/10e chambre: Instants d'audience* (2004, 105 min.), and *Emergencies/Urgences* (1988, 105 min.). These laboratories of modernity seem in stark contrast to the desert landscapes, fields, and French farmyards represented elsewhere in his film and photographic *œuvre*. However, Depardon's images – and writing – consistently draw on personal stories and memories to meditate on the image itself, on what it represents, reflects, excludes, and the responsibilities its composition and circulation confers on its maker. In films such as *Empty Quarter: A Woman in Africa/Empty Quarter, une femme en Afrique* (1985, 90 min.), *La Captive du désert* (1990, 90 min.), and the *Profils paysans* trilogy, for example, the lateral framing of open spaces, the informality of narrative structures, the concern with difference and change that characterises the framing are directly influenced by existential concerns.[24] There is more than enough of everywhere in *San Clemente*, just as the defiant farmers from the Cévennes region share more than one might think with the nomads and peasant workers of North Africa and South-East Asia. Possibly, the tensions and paradoxes that have characterised Depardon's work since the 1970s (here/there, document/fiction, image/text, anchor/relay, objective/subjective) issue from the traveller's desire to rediscover the whereabouts of home: 'I don't regret my many pictures of Brigitte Bardot. It's just that I would have liked to have a good one of my father.'[25]

Depardon's New York photographs were subsequently published in two books, *Correspondance new-yorkaise* (1981), and *Manhattan Out* (2008). The first was compiled from a (daily) photographic commission for *Libération* during the summer of 1981, and it includes an epilogue which comprises photographs of his family farm, and a critical essay by Alain Bergala. The second comprises black-and-white street photographs taken by Depardon in the winter of 1980, photographs he had originally disregarded.[26] Hoping to capture his subjects unawares, he had photographed them from the waist and hip without using the viewfinder. The resultant images of people walking, jogging, colliding, roller-skating, cycling, falling over, and getting arrested are frequently set against either diverting background activity, or the Manhattan skyline. Many of the subjects are decked in large overcoats and thick winter furs, others hide under their hoods (reminiscent of the figures in *San Clemente*), a man strolls towards the camera wearing a balaclava, another (with plasters on his nose and ear, and a bottle of champagne in his coat pocket) glances nonchalantly at the photographer. Initially, Depardon felt there was nothing particularly distinctive or unusual about these photographs. He felt he hadn't made 'contact' with Manhattan, and possibly, when set against the contemporary New York street photography of people like Tod Papageorge and Helen Levitt – not to mention the more iconic work of Lee Friedlander, Garry Winogrand, Weegee, or Diane Arbus – he had failed to adapt his photojournalistic and reportage skills to the city. Twenty-seven years later, Depardon came across the photographs in a storage box and to his amazement they were not at all as he remembered them: 'It's interesting to realize that most Americans I captured on photo were looking at the lens and were therefore aware of their picture being taken ... I was convinced at the time that I had them fooled.'[27] It is this experience of Manhattan as an outsider, a wanderer, which also explains the history of his *Ten Minutes Silence for John Lennon*.

In contrast to *Happy Birthday to John*, Depardon's film is composed almost entirely of a single circular panning shot taken from a fixed position somewhere in the crowd. More reminiscent of his first foray into documentary filmmaking, *Ian Palach* (1969, col., 12 min.) than his later experiments with 'direct cinema' techniques (e.g. *Numéros zero* (1977, col., 90 min.)), the framing formations in *Ten Minutes Silence* are a product of Depardon's changing sense of what the camera can capture unawares, unexpected, from the incidental reality of an unfolding event. The film begins abruptly just over two minutes into the vigil with a shot of the crowd. A man squats in the foreground wearing a dark-green beret, white scarf, and gloves. He occupies the bottom right quarter of the frame. He is bearded and wears a pair of small, round dark spectacles. The camera meets his stillness. He seems unaware of its presence but we can't be certain, and neither is the filmmaker. As with the images in *Manhattan Out*, it is difficult to know who is performing to the camera and who is not, who is posing by not posing. The man's general appearance resembles that of Lennon, as does the appearance of any number of people drawn into Depardon's frame throughout the film.

As the hand-held camera tracks along its path, other figures come into view. A woman wearing a long, red overcoat also features in this opening frame, head down and hands clasped in silent prayer. Again, as the camera continues to pan left, we notice the assertive presence of red (a coat, hat, scarf, badge, paper cup). Although there are no titles at the beginning, at the end the film title does appear in bold red lettering across a long shot of the dispersing crowd. Red also dominates the *mise en scène* of *Ian Palach*, although the metaphorical connotations are more obvious in that case. As with Mekas's films, the more Depardon's documentary lens tries to be innocent, the more unrehearsed repetitions, coincidences, patterns of colour and demeanour manifest themselves. Medium close-ups of individual mourners invariably give way to images of larger groups, or clusters of mourners, before coming to rest again on a different individual. Filmed at some distance from the park's Bandshell, there seems to be no obvious central attraction with people looking in various directions, some swaying gently with the breeze, others struggle to remain motionless, and observant. Some find the silence uncomfortable, and dislike Depardon's voyeurism. For others, his probing camera momentarily fills the void, somewhere else to look.

Opposing the prevailing breeze, the camera continues to move left. Two men now dominate the foreground. One is looking upwards, the other wears a Stetson and appears to be either saluting or just holding his hat in place, or both. Avoiding the scrutiny – or intrusion – of the camera, a red-haired man in a sleeveless flak jacket turns away and the camera obligingly tilts downwards, as if in embarrassment. The dry leaves of late autumn come into fuller view, before the Manhattan skyline rises in the background. A man sits on the leaf-covered ground, beside him is another man wearing a

14   *Ten Minutes Silence for John Lennon/Dix minutes de silence pour John Lennon*

red bandana. Trees appear, with figures sitting and standing on their branches. Off-screen a camera clicks somewhere, and in the background someone fidgets with a paper bag. These sudden sounds do not end the silence; rather, they interrupt the extremely loud drone of the helicopter hovering overhead. Casually, the camera pans slightly to the right and then slowly makes its way upwards, past the trees and across the skyline into a patch of clear sky where the helicopter momentarily comes into view.[28] The sequence ends with the generalised sound of applause and cheering as a recording of 'Imagine' begins playing over the PA system, followed by a long shot of the crowds leaving the park. As in *Happy Birthday to John*, *Ten Minutes Silence for John Lennon* ends in a strangely uplifting, celebratory, mood.

In both films categorical distinctions between the factual and the rhetorical, objectivity and intimacy, between journalistic, diaristic, and eulogistic motives and forms, dissolve amid the realities of the events being filmed. *Happy Birthday to John* demythologises Lennon and its flickering images and shadow plays convey the fragility of a life, and the absurdity of its fame. It also never finds Lennon: throughout, he remains impossibly elusive, not so much untouchable as unreachable, and already absent. The film may begin with his voice, but its stream of images and sounds only ever captures a figure performing, posing, strangely awkward, vulnerable, and essentially uncomfortable with whatever world happens to be around him (interviews, exhibitions, parties, concerts). For Depardon too, the event being filmed remains elusive, endlessly slipping and falling out of the frame, there but not there. Ultimately, if these films are elegies to anything, it is to the fantasy of representing reality, and that, finally, is what makes their journey to Central Park a journey worth making.

Notes

1   E. B. White, *Here Is New York* (New York: Little Bookroom, 1999), p. 26.

2   The economic decline and social disintegration of New York in the mid 1970s is the subject of two Rudy Burckhardt films from this era: *Default Averted* (1975, b&w, 20 min.), *Sodom and Gomorrha* (1976, col., 6 min.). Chantal Akerman's *News From Home* (1977, 16 mm, Fr./Bel., 89 min.) also offers a fascinating portrait of the city at this time.

3   For data and discussion on New York City during this period, see John Hull Mollenkopf, 'The Post-Industrial Transformation of the Political Order in New York City', in his *Power, Culture, and Place: Essays on New York City* (New York: Russell Sage Foundation, 1988), pp. 223–58; and his *New York City in the 1980s: A Social, Economic, and Political Atlas* (New York: Simon & Schuster, 1993). Vincent J. Cannato offers a revisionist analysis in his essay, 'Bright Lights, Doomed Cities: The Rise or Fall of New York City in the 1980s', in *Living in the Eighties*, eds Gil Troy and Vincent J. Cannato (Oxford: Oxford University Press, 2009), pp. 70–84.

4   George Melly, 'John Lennon [1980]', in *The Lennon Companion: Twenty-Five Years of Comment*, eds Elizabeth Thompson and David Gutman (London: Macmillan, 1987), p. 226.

5   For a discussion of media responses to Lennon's death, particu-
    larly the US print media, see Fred Fogo, *'I Read the News': The
    Social Drama of John Lennon's Death* (Lanham, MD: Rowan &
    Littlefield, 1994). Anthony Elliott's *The Mourning of John Lennon*
    (Berkeley, CA: University California Press, 1999) is a compre-
    hensive study of Lennon's death and its socio-psychological
    effects.

6   Philip Norman, *John Lennon: The Life* (London: Harper, 2008),
    p. 264.

7   Scott MacDonald, '[Interview with] Jonas Mekas [1982/83]', *A
    Critical Cinema: 2: Interviews with Independent Filmmakers*, Vol. 2
    (Berkeley, CA: University of California Press, 1992), p. 101. On
    the relations between Mekas's diaristic method and other (mod-
    ernist) documentary forms, see Michael Renov's *'Lost, Lost, Lost*:
    Mekas as Essayist', *The Subject of Documentary* (Minneapolis,
    MN: University of Minnesota Press, 2004), pp. 69–91.

8   Bryan Fry, 'Me, I Just Film My Life: An Interview with Jonas
    Mekas', *Senses of Cinema*, 44 (2007), http://archive.sensesofcin-
    ema.com/contents/07/44/jonas-mekas-interview.html

9   Maureen Turim, 'Reminiscences, Subjectivities, and Truths', in
    To Free the Cinema: Jonas Mekas and the New York Underground,
    ed. David E. James (Princeton, NJ: Princeton University Press,
    1992), p. 211.

10 Arthur C. Danto, *Unnatural Wonders: Essays from the Gap between
    Art and Life* (New York: Columbia University Press, 2005),
    p. 337.

11 On Fluxus, see Hannah Higgins's *Fluxus Experience* (Berkeley,
    CA: University of California Press, 2002); Ken Fiedman, ed.,
    The Fluxus Reader (Chichester: Academic Editions/John Wiley,
    1998). On Maciunas, see Geoffrey Henricks, 'The Flux-Mass
    of George Maciunas', in *Critical Mass: Happenings, Performance,
    Fluxus, Intermedia, and Rutgers University: 1958–1972* (New
    Brunswick, NJ: Rutgers University Press, 2003), pp. 130–40.

12 Danto, *Unnatural Wonders*, p. 345. In March 1965, the Maysles
    brothers filmed Ono peforming *Cut Piece* at the Carnegie Hall.

13 See Scott MacDonald's '[Interview with] Yoko Ono [1989]'
    in *A Critical Cinema: 2*, pp. 139–56; and his 'Yoko Ono: *No.
    4 (Bottoms)*', in *Avant-Garde Film: Motion Studies*, ed. Scott
    MacDonald (Cambridge: Cambridge University Press, 1993), pp.
    19–27.

14 Danto, *Unnatural Wonders*, pp. 70–1.

15   Jon Wiener, 'Pop and Avant-Garde: The Case of John and Yoko', *Popular Music and Society*, 22.1 (1998), p. 3.

16   The Japanese experimental filmmaker and Fluxus member, Takahiko Limura, also made a film featuring this press conference and exhibition: *Yoko Ono: This Is Not Here* (1999, Lux (VHS/NTSC), 19 min.). Mekas's inter-title gives 1972 as the year of this exhibition at Everson but this is incorrect, as is the date given for the party at Allen Klein's house (12 June 1971) – which was held either a week after the Everson exhibition, or on 6 July 1971. Some of Mekas's footage from this party is also included in *Gimme Some Truth: The Making of John Lennon's* Imagine *Album* (Andrew Solt, 2000, 60 min.). The date given in the film for the Central Park vigil (8 December) is in fact the date of Lennon's death. Sean Kirst, 'Imagine: John and Yoko at the Everson and Hotel', *Post-Standard*, 8 December 2005, http://syracusethenandnow.org/Dwntwn/Columbus/HotelSyracuse/JohnYokoHotlSyr.htm

17   Norman, *John Lennon*, pp. 699–700; see also Jon Wiener's *Come Together: John Lennon in His Time* (New York: Random House, 1984).

18   See also Scott MacDonald's *The Garden in the Machine: A Field Guide to Independent Films about Place* (Berkeley, CA: University of California Press, 2001), pp. 223–46.

19   Raymond Depardon, *Manhattan Out* (Guttenberg: Steidl, 2009), npg.

20   Depardon, *Notes* (Paris: Éditions Arfuyen, 1979).

21   Depardon, *Voyages* (Paris: Hazan, 1998), p. 594.

22   Depardon, *Manhattan Out*, npg.

23   Depardon, *Voyages*, pp. 398–9.

24   Depardon's *Profils paysans* series comprises three films documenting the changing pace and appearance of life in the Cévennes region: *L'approache* (2001, 88 min.); *Le quotidian* (2005, 90 min.); and *La vie moderne/Modern Life* (2008, 88 min.).

25   Depardon, *Our Farm* (Arles: Actes Sud, 2006), p. 304.

26   Depardon (with Alain Bergala), *Correspondance New-Yorkaise* (Paris: Libération/Éditions de l'Étoile, 1981). He subsequently made a short film, *New York, N.Y.* (1984, b&w, 10 min.), which comprised three sequence shots (taken at dawn, midday, night). The first is taken from inside the elevated railcar heading to Brooklyn, the second is a shot of commuters walking on a street, and the final shot is again taken from inside the railcar but this time returning to Manhattan. The film has a particularly

memorable soundtrack comprising sirens, footsteps, car horns, and silence.

27   Depardon, *Manhattan Out*, npg.

28   A live 'Eyewitness Report Special' of the vigil was broadcast by WABC-TV Channel 7 NYC, introduced by Roger Grimsby, and with a hapless Ernie Anastos reporting from Central Park (shivering, confused about dates, and referring at one point to Ono as Lennon's 'late widow'). At time of writing, it was still possible to watch the entire programme on YouTube, including the shots of Central Park – perhaps, shots taken from the same helicopter that Depardon films from the ground in *Ten Minutes Silence*: www.youtube.com/watch?v=v_h_ZUh5QX4 [accessed 31/03/2010].

7

Architectures of vision

> LXIII. We
> talked about Gaudí.   Mies van der Rohe
> admired the Gaudí buildings in and near
> Barcelona and the Park Güell.   Laura
> said that driving to the apartment
> from the office Mies was
> misanthropic.   He had said that there are
> too few good people in the world.
> (John Cage, 'Diary: How to Improve the World, 1967')[1]

In May 1962, at Tokyo's Sōgetsu Arts Centre (SAC), Yoko Ono gave a solo performance comprising music, poems, 'instructions for paintings', and 'a piece for chairs'. It was part of a programme of events featuring work by contemporary artists who were active in conceptual art and neo-Dadaist circles at that time. The programme also included the work of John Cage, and caused the first tremors of so-called 'Cage-Shock' to reverberate through Japan's avant-garde community. Ono had initially met Cage in New York, through her marriage to Toshi Ichiyanagi (one of his former students), and he had attended the Chambers Street 'loft concerts' she had organised with La Monte Young. Other associates of Cage who performed in that 1962–64 season at SAC included David Tudor, Robert Rauschenberg, Jasper Johns, Nam June Paik, and the dancer-choreographers Merce Cunningham and Jean Erdman. Although less controversial than the annual Yomiuri Independent Exhibition, the programmes at SAC were similarly influenced by the widespread opposition to the renewal of the US–Japan Security Treaty (Anpo tōsō) in 1960. William Klein – whose *Broadway by Light* (1959) was screened at SAC in 1961 – photographed Tokyo at that time, and his images convey a still frantic, vulnerable metropolis, caught between dazed disquiet and rampant redevelopment.[2] In particular, SAC emerged as the principal venue for artistic collaborations between Tokyo-based artists and their (predominantly) New York counterparts, and the place where Cage's aesthetics of indeterminacy – not to mention his Zen Buddhism – readily coincided with the activities of groups such as Gutai ('Embodiment'), Zero Dimension, Voice of the Voiceless, and Hi Red Centre (which George Maciunas would soon invite into the Fluxus fold).[3]

SAC was a relatively recent addition to the Sōgetsu Kaikan complex, where adequate space for screenings, concerts, and art exhibitions had only become available when the School moved into its new Kenzō Tange-designed building in 1958. Since the late 1920s, the Sōgetsu had been associated with its founding master (*iemoto*), Sōfū Teshigahara, whose freestyle approach to floral art (*ikebana*) was strongly influenced by European modernism. An accomplished painter, sculptor, and calligrapher in his own right, Sōfū reconceived *ikebana* as a conceptual – rather than an ornamental – art form, integrating found objects into his works (e.g. pieces of coloured glass, broken ceramics, stones, bits of driftwood, and discarded metal, etc.) in a manner not dissimilar to Cornell's assemblage techniques, or even Cage's practice of dropping nuts and bolts into a piano. Rather than reproducing decorative colour and textural arrangements, Sōfū's works were often dramatic, exposing broken branches and roots, and emphasising the essential particularity of each artwork's found and fabricated elements.[4] Sōfū had travelled to Europe in the 1930s, spending time studying the methods of contemporary artists like Giorgio de Chirico, Picasso, Dalí, and Joan Miró. After the Second World War, his style of *ikebana* increasingly came under the influence of Abstract Expressionism, and he became enthusiastic about the role of intuition, spontaneity, and 'action' in nurturing an authentically modern Japanese visual culture. Although works by Jackson Pollock, Mark Rothko, Mark Tobey, and others, had been exhibited in Japan during the Occupation period (at the Yorimuri in 1951, for example), Sōfū was also drawn to its French counterpart, the Art Informel movement, and the ideas of its foremost curator and intellectual, Michel Tapié. Throughout the 1950s and 1960s, Tapié was instrumental in arranging exhibitions of contemporary Japanese art in Europe and the US, especially at the Martha Jackson Gallery in Manhattan. At SAC, meanwhile, 'the audience seats were flanked by large [2 x 8 m] paintings by Georges Mathieu [*Bataille de Hakata*] and Sam Francis [*Tokyo Mural*] – respectively representing European Art Informel and American Abstract Expressionism – emblematic of the centre's internationalist ambition and orientation', an ethos that also appealed to Sōfū's filmmaker son, Hiroshi, who assumed responsibility for SAC in 1959, and programmed most of its events throughout the next decade.[5]

ikebana/cinema

Documentary films, I soon concluded, are not necessarily the means of recording or reflecting reality. They could be the ideal medium for expressing the director's philosophy as well. (Hiroshi Teshigahara)[6]

While Hiroshi Teshigahara shared his father's enthusiasm for modernism, he had less sympathy for his social conservatism. While studying painting at the Tokyo School of Fine Arts in the immediate post-war period, Hiroshi associated with communist and anarchist activists, supporting their opposition to the brutal methods adopted by the Allied Occupation Force authorities and Japan's newly constituted democracy to repress strikes, and demonstrations against the prevailing US/UN policy towards Korea. Radical artists and intellectuals (such as Tarō Okamoto, Kiyoteru Hanada, and Shūzō Takiguchi) taught at the university,[7] and also helped to organise underground groups to discuss theories of modern art, and the relations between art, literature, music and contemporary politics. At these meetings, Teshigahara struck up friendships with people who would collaborate with him throughout his later filmmaking career – most notably, Kōbō Abe (writer), and

Tōru Takemitsu (composer). It was also during this period that he began to explore the expressive possibilities of photography and film.

As his enthusiasm for oil painting waned, he recognised in documentary film a medium that was not only at the forefront of contemporary aesthetic debates about reality and its representations, but one also open to collaborative experimentation with other art forms. This change in direction was also encouraged by his association with groups that vigorously promoted the virtues of 'total art' and the blurring of boundaries between the traditional arts, groups such as Okamoto's and Hanada's *Yoru no Kai* (Society of the Night), *Seikin no Kai* (Century Society), and *Jikken Kōbō* (Experimental Workshop); Takemitsu was a leading member of this latter group, and its work provided the template for the contemporary music programmes at SAC throughout the 1960s. Teshigahara's commitment to filmmaking was further affirmed in 1955, when he began working as an editor, and then assistant director, to Fumio Kamei, the radical pacifist and communist; and when he co-founded the Cinema 57 group, with Susumu Hani, who also made several modernist documentaries at this time exploring the relations between art and education (*Children Who Draw/Eo kaku kodomotachi* (1955, JP, 16 mm, b&w and col., 38 min.)), and sculpture (*Horyuji* (1958, JP, b&w, 22 min.)). Cinema 57 dedicated itself to screening new, independent Japanese cinema, and – like Takemitsu's 'Experimental Workshop' – became assimilated into SAC.

Throughout the 1950s, Teshigahara made several documentaries that reflected his wider interest in the visual arts. As the decade progressed, he drifted from the radical politics espoused by Hanada and Kamei, turning instead – as Kōbō Abe had done in the late 1940s – to the existentialist writing of western intellectuals such as Karl Jaspers and Jean-Paul Sartre. He also became increasingly attracted to the idea of using the basement in the new Sōgetsu Kaikan complex as a venue for hosting multimedia performances and exhibitions, as well as film screenings. In 1953, he had directed *Hokusai* (JP, b&w, 23 min.), a short tableau-style documentary about the life and work of the renowned Edo period *ukiyo-e* woodblock master, whose 'The Great Wave off Kanagawa' print – from his *Thirty-Six Views of Mount Fuji* (1825–35) series – is particularly well known in the West. Championed by fin de siècle Japanophiles like Edmond de Goncourt and Siegfried 'Samuel' Bing, Hokusai's prints became key works for the *Japonisme* movement, and had an important influence on Impressionist and post-Impressionist art, including that of Santiago Rusiñol and Herman Anglada-Camarasa, and other figures associated with Catalan *modernisme*. For the most part, Teshigahara's film, however, animates images from the earlier sketches and ink drawings (especially, the *Hokusai Manga* collection), at times closing in on a particular face, or feature, but always conveying the busy, eventful world of the period. When the film does turn its attentions to Hokusai's familiar depictions of Mount Fuji, they appear to the audience within a more historically nuanced context, somewhat removed – or retrieved – from the orientalist excesses of *Japonisme*. Although Teshigahara had originally secured this project by chance, its importance within his film *œuvre* should not be underestimated, especially in relation to *Antonio Gaudí* (1984, JP, 72 min.).

Other documentary projects from the 1950s also evince Teshigahara's evolving visual style, and commitment to working between film and other arts, for example: *The Twelve Photographers/Juuninin no shashinka* (1955, JP, b&w, 49 min.), and *Tokyo 1958* (1958, JP, b&w, 24 min.), both of which were collaborative projects involving contributions from photographers, critics, and other filmmakers (including Hani). *Tokyo 1958* is especially noteworthy as a satirical documentary that includes stop-motion animation and collage effects in its wry commentary on Japan's consumerist capital. Using images from the works of Hokusai and Kitagawa Utamaro, it superimposes hand-painted cut-outs and stop-motion effects on *actualité* footage of downtown Tokyo. Influenced by both surrealism and street photography, the film juxtaposes two Tokyos: one contemporary and post-occupation, buoyant after hosting the Asian Games that year, and busy with commuters, consumers, and visitors; while the other, evokes the era of the Tokugawa shogunate, setting the pre-modern inside the contemporary, the unresolved questions of Japanese history against the contemporary stampede towards modernity.

Teshigahara's most aesthetically ambitious and technically accomplished documentary from the 1950s is *Ikebana* (1956, JP, 32 min.). Ostensibly, a film about the Sōgetsu School, and the teachings of Sōfū in particular, it develops into a carefully arranged set of filmic ruminations on art, life, work, and impermanence. The film's opening title sequence, for example, showcases the Sōgetsu philosophy of *ikebana*, by juxtaposing conventional Japanese calligraphic script with abstract lines and squiggles. It then opens with a shot of a train approaching and passing. This is followed by an establishing shot of an apartment block before cutting to several close-ups of chrysanthemums in bloom. A young woman begins carefully picking flowers before returning to her apartment to create an *ikebana* arrangement, which is then framed within (the frame of) an alcove. Again, the sequences are structured around a series of juxtapositions: the shot of the train may allude to the Lumières' *L'arrivée d'un train en gare de La Ciotat*, and/or the contemporary films of Ozu – and, therefore, to the cinema itself. In these opening sequences, flowers, and the art of their arrangement, replace machines and motion, as the naturalistic soundtrack also fades behind a voice-over reciting lines from *The Pillow Book/Makura no Sōshi*, an *anthology* of reflections, observations, and reminiscences by a Heian period imperial lady-in-waiting, Sei Shōnagon (and a book that also features in Chris Marker's *Sunless/Sans Soleil* (1983, Fr., 99 min.)). The film then changes from this series of visual associations to a narrated outline history of *ikebana*, illustrated – in the manner of *Hokusai* – through a montage of paintings, prints, and decorative panels (mainly, from the eighteenth and nineteenth centuries). Like the changing seasons, the film then cuts to 'live action', as two women, working in the Sōgetsu School, demonstrate their art, and its essentially ceremonial nature. This traditional aspect of *ikebana* – its Zen provenance, and relations to other Japanese rituals, especially the tea ceremonies – is also enunciated in the next sequence, which comprises a series of shots of the Ginkakuji temple, and its gardens, with the 'Sea of Silver Sand'. All of which culminates with the first appearance of Sōfū, busily preparing for his annual exhibition, and whose teachings and artworks dominate much of rest of the film.

Even a cursory analysis of these opening sequences from *Ikebana* shows Teshigahara's increasingly fluent use of a visually distinctive documentary language, and his ability to articulate meaning through different forms, montage configurations, and contrasts. His highly expressive use of the cut, for example, has a particular resonance within *ikebana*, where the 'cut' (*kire*) is crucial to the arrangement and preservation of each individual flower. As with *Nō* choreography, the syllabic structures of the *haiku*, or even, perhaps, Yoko Ono's *Cut Piece* (which was first performed at SAC in 1964), the cut interrupts continuity (*suzuki*) to transcend it, to draw attention to the inviolable uniqueness of things, transience as a sign of permanence, death as always a beginning. As the contemporary Dutch philosopher of aesthetics, Henk Oosterling puts it:

> *Ikebana* ... is most literally based on precise cutting. In artificially arranging the freshly cut flowers, nature is exposed. Through cutting, life comes to full bloom. It is the arrangement that creates naturalness. In stylization nature and culture, original and copy, impulse and mediation, being and appearance, organism and technique coincide ... By *kire* nature unfolds itself.[8]

The film's carefully arranged series of sequences create a space into which Sōfū enters, and with him the methods and metaphysics of *ikebana*. Throughout, scenes of Sōfū at work are juxtaposed with shots of various completed *ikebana* artworks and sculptures. In one sequence, for example, Sōfū is framed in a reverse shot, staring at a large, empty (blank) bonsai tray. Using rudimentary but vivid special effects, abstract strips, fragments, blocks of primary colours suddenly congregate above the tray, animating the artist's creative process – an artist who thinks chiefly in terms of colour and space. The film closes with tracking shots of Sōfū's larger sculptures, made from various materials, and situated or exhibited on a beach, as the sun sets and the seawater washes ashore. This sequence again evokes images of cutting and continuity, of art crossing real and imaginary boundaries: the land and the sea, life and death, past and present.

In the film's final sequence, current political preoccupations are inserted into the *mise en scène*. The camera closes in on one of Sōfū's large skull-like stone sculptures, situated on a desolate beach and facing the setting sun (images of skulls and intimations of mortality recur throughout the film). In another example of basic trick cinematography, Teshigahara superimposes on one of the sculpture's 'eyes' an excerpt from the US War Department archival footage of the bombing of Hiroshima. In wake of the 'Bikini incident' in 1954, when a crew of over twenty fishermen was exposed to fallout from a US thermonuclear test on Bikini Atoll, anti-nuclear – and anti-US – political opinion had intensified in Japan.[9] Often under the aegis of the Japan Council Against Atomic and Hydrogen Bombs, figures such as Fumio Kamei were engaged to produce compelling documentaries advocating unilateral disarmament, and he co-directed some of these films with Teshigahara, including *The World Is Terrified: The Nature of the 'Ash of Death'/Sekai wa kyōfu suru: Shi no hai no shōtai* (1957, JP, b&w, 79 min.).

Teshigahara/Gaudí

> Those who have not heard the chromatic, glowing stridence of his colour, the striking polyphony of his organ-pipe towers, and the clash of his mutating decorative naturalism, are traitors because they intentionally ignore the essential role of colour, light, sounds, and silence in Gaudí's work. (Salvador Dalí)[10]

In 1959, Tapié arranged for a selection of Sōfū's wood sculptures to be exhibited in Manhattan. Teshigahara decided to accompany his father on this trip, which would also involve a sojourn in Europe. While in New York, he made another 16 mm documentary, *José Torres* (1959, JP, b&w, 25 min.). Impressed by the US hand-held, photojournalistic style of the times, the film and its subject matter quickly became another experiment with form: attentively observing the life of a rising professional boxer, originally from Puerto Rico, living and training in the backstreets. In particular, this film gave him an opportunity to learn an alternative cinematographic style, a style that would – in its immediacy and black-and-white austerity – inform his creative relationship with Hiroshi Segawa, the principal cinematographer on the collaborations with Kōbō Abe, collaborations that would later secure Teshigahara's international reputation as a major Japanese director.[11] Just as the *mise en scène* of *José Torres* registers the influence of journalism and direct cinema, so too Takemitsu's score for the film complements its vernacular approach to framing and editing by fusing orchestral jazz (and citing Leonard Bernstein's compositions for *West Side Story*, which had opened on Broadway in 1957) with a more improvisational, free jazz style. Interestingly, Teshigahara returned to New York in 1965 to make a second documentary on Torres, this time covering preparations for his world championship fight against Willie Pastrono. Like Klein's Muhammad Ali films from this era, *José Torres: Part II* is also a documentary about the business of boxing, and its shady world of impresarios, officials, and managers. It also – more explicitly than *José Torres: Part I* – configures boxing as the quintessential US metaphor, and includes the presence of its pre-eminent intellectual of the day, Norman Mailer.

After New York, Sōfū and his party headed to Europe, where Teshigahara was introduced to Barcelona, and the world of Gaudí. While he claimed to be 'totally unprepared for the intense shock of this encounter with [Gaudí's] architecture', it is quite possible that Teshigahara's stay in New York had already primed him for this revelation.[12] In the winter of 1957–58, for example, MoMA had mounted a major international exhibition of Gaudí's work (comprising intricate architectural models, casts, photographs, and other artefacts). Dalí participated in a symposium held during the exhibition, along with Josep Lluís Sert (the exiled Catalonian architect and academic, who had recently become dean of the Harvard Graduate School of Design). In 1960, Praeger published a book based on the exhibition, with a cover designed by Miró. In that same year, George R. Collins's seminal book on Gaudí was published to coincide with the founding of the Gaudí Archive

15   *Antonio Gaudí*: Casa Milá (Pedrera)

at Columbia University. It is unlikely that any curious artist
visiting and exhibiting in Manhattan during the late 1950s
would have been unaware of the flurry of curatorial and critical
activity surrounding Gaudí's work at that time. It was certainly
of interest to Tapié, who, in due course, would produce a book
on Gaudí's Casa Milá – a building behind which, according to
Gijs van Hensbergen, 'there is an oriental aesthetic seen in the
popular prints by Hokusai'.[13]

Teshigahara made two documentary films in Barcelona with
Gaudí's work as their subject. The first, *Gaudí, Catalunya,
1959* (2008 [1959], JP, 16 mm, 19 min.) comprises footage shot
during the visit with his father and Tapié; the second is the
better known and widely released feature-length documentary,
Antonio Gaudí. The first seems a sketch or reconnoitre for the
second, the impressions of a tourist-filmmaker excited by new
sights, discoveries, and encounters (it contains the original
footage of their meeting with Dalí at his home in Portlligat,
for example). Although the second film was made with consid-

erably more resources, it is a sequel to – rather than a realisation of – the first Gaudí film. These films belong to two very different periods in Teshigahara's career, periods separated by the halcyon days of SAC, the teratology of film collaborations with Kōbō Abe, Japan's post-occupation 'economic miracle', the death of Sōfū (in 1979), and Horoshi's new role as the (not unreluctant) successor to his father's role as head of the Sōgestu School.

As in *Hokusai* and *Ikebana*, *Antonio Gaudí* begins with a series or montage of short sequences that establish a formal and social background for the film's principal subject. It opens with a wide shot of the Font màgica de Montjuïc (Magic Fountain of Montjuïc), erupting into soaring jets of water, colour, and noise, during one of the night-time performances – an image that also evokes Teshigahara's extraordinary 'flowing' bamboo installations from the 1990s. It then cuts to softer-focus shots of Barcelona's Barri Gòtic (Gothic Quarter) in the early morning, compositions that accentuate the narrow, enclosed, verticality of the old town. This juxtaposition of times and spaces is immediately followed by another sequence in which the camera patiently tracks the Picasso friezes on the façade at the entrance to El Col·legi d'Arquitectes de Catalunya (Architects' Association of Catalonia) building. From this example of public art celebrating the city's history of art, Teshigahara then moves to others: a shot of Miró's promenade mosaic in the Ramblas, and several of Antoni Tàpies' remarkable object-assemblage, 'Tribute to Picasso'/'Homenatge a Picasso' (1981–83). Takemitsu's soundtrack then falls silent as the Plaça Sant Felip Neri (Plaza de Sant Felip Neri) appears on the screen. The camera slowly circles the deserted plaza, framing the pock-marked, damaged walls of its church, and conveying its strange equanimity. The soundtrack then bursts into traditional Catalan music as the film cuts to shots of citizens, standing in circles in the square, holding hands and dancing the *sardana*. A more sombre mood returns as the film then shifts to a series of images from the Museu Naciona d'Art de Catalunya, images of religious paintings, frescoes, relics, and statues from the museum's collection of medieval art. With remarkable cinematic economy, Teshigahara then invokes the legacy of Catalan *modernisme* with a sequence of shots comprising views of Lluís Domenech's Palau de la Música Catalana (Palace of Catalan Music), Salvador Valeri i Pupurull's Casa Comalat, and Josep Puig i Cadafalch's Casa Amatller, bringing this opening segment to a close, as the film then pulls back to frame both the Casa Amatller and the building beside it: Gaudí's Casa Batlló.

This overture of fragments, a tableau of impressions and juxtapositions also constitutes a particular history of Barcelona, a history that belongs to – and still defines – Gaudí's architecture. It connects the city's experience of war with that of other cities (such as Tokyo, perhaps). Interestingly, the segment begins and ends by referring not to Gaudí but to the work of his *modernista* contemporary, Puig i Cadafalch. Ahead of the second Barcelona 'Expo' in 1929, Primo de Rivera's anti-regionalist Spanish government controversially demolished Puig i Cadafalch's 'The Four Columns'/'Les Quatre Columnes' (a monument celebrating Catalan national identity, which had been erected in 1919), and replaced it with the Magic Fountain. The marks and holes in the walls surrounding the Plaça Sant Felip Neri were made during the Civil War when the Fascists bombed it, killing forty-two people (mostly children) who were hiding in the church – the same church Gaudí had been walking towards in 1926, when he was accidentally hit by a tram, and killed. The *sardana* – which also features in *Gaudí, Catalunya, 1959* – is a deeply political activity; the national dance of Catalonia, it was censured by the regimes of both Primo de Rivera and Franco. The late medieval art that features in the film depicts scenes of torture and religious persecution, relating to Barcelona's role in the Spanish Inquisition, and the massacre of Catalonia's Jewish population. These images simultaneously evoke antiquity and modernity, and their traces are present in the art of Picasso and Dalí. Throughout this opening segment, then, relations between shots and sequences are associative rather than expository, creating a pattern of contrasts that extend the formal and allegorical scope of the images, asserting from the onset that this documentary will not present or exhibit Gaudí's work in any simplistic and realist way.

Like Tokyo, Barcelona's geography is defined by its proximity to mountains, and the sea. Impressions of water, gathering waves, and maritime motifs are a recurrent feature of Gaudí's style, and Teshigahara's camera fixes on these details until they seem abstract, and free to transcend the immediate environment. Close-ups of the wave-patterned and seashell mouldings on the ceilings of the Casa Milà, and frontal shots of its undulating roof, for example, correspond with later images in the film, such as those of the Sagrada Família School, and the fish stalls at the Boquería. The *Nautilus*-like interior of the Casa Batlló is further invoked in the montage of interchanging perspectives used to represent the Casa Milà's balconies, with their wrought-iron ribbons of seaweed, and Takemitsu's soundtrack – which includes actual sounds of the sea. Meanwhile, images of Montserrat – and its distinctive rock formations – reappear in the coarse textures and rugged shapes created by the clinker bricks Gaudí used in the construction of the road bridge and galleries at Parc Güell, or the walls of the chapel at Colonia Güell. Such images also contrast with the sublime curves, parabolic arches, and smooth plasterwork found elsewhere in Gaudí's buildings, interiors, and furnishings. By including sequences of rural Catalonia or the busy Boquería market (the present), or old photographs and architectural drawings (the past), the film reminds its audience of the complexity of contexts, and how the achievements of an artist like Gaudí invariably transcend typical aesthetic and cultural categories. Like an *ikebana* sculpture, *Antonio Gaudí* is arranged around images of contrasting shapes and textures, natural and artificial forms, alternate tracking and framing configurations, and how – in its final segment – this intricate, reflexive documentary *mise en scène* becomes a filmic homage to Gaudí's remarkable – and famously still unfinished – cathedral, the Sagrada Família.

In cinematically translating its subject into the language of *ikebana*, the film also generates a myriad of possible parallels between the cultures of Catalonia and Japan. For example, it contains numerous close shots of Gaudí's extensive use of the

16   *Antonio Gaudí*: Sagrada Família

broken tiles (*trencadissos*) in decorating ventilator covers and
chimneys (e.g. the Casa Milà, and especially, the Palau Güell),
or the benches of the Parc Güell, a practice resembling the
traditional Japanese ceramic art of *kintsugi*. Recurrent images
of circles, spirals, and whirlpools (including the *sardana*) in
the film evoke the symbolic circles in Buddhism, especially the
hand-drawn *ensō*, which connotes the momentary detachment
of body and spirit. While the significance of the dragon in
Catalan culture usually relates to its patron saint (Sant Jordi),
in Gaudí's case its presence in the roof design for the Casa
Batlló, and the gates of the Pavellons Güell (Güell Pavilions),
is a tribute to the contemporary Catalan nationalist poet,
Jacint Verdaguer, whose epic poem, *L'Atlàntida* (1876), retells
Hercules' slaying of the dragon. Although more commonly
associated with Chinese culture, images of dragons and sala-
manders are also ubiquitous in Japanese woodblock prints, and
at Buddhist temples and Shinto shrines.
    As befits an architect so engrossed in what he called 'the

great book of nature', Gaudí's method often involved adapting botanical – especially, arboreal – structures and designs: the most astonishing example of which being the tree-trunk columns and pillars, and their supporting branch-like systems, in the Sagrada Família. Teshigahara not only uses the documentary form to explore this aspect of Gaudí's style, he renders it through the eyes of *ikebana*, as in, for example: the low-angle shots of plant-crowned balustrades along the viaduct at Parc Güell; the floral stained-glass windows in the Colònia Güell Crypt; the bamboo garden and oriental fountain at Palau Reial de Pedralbes; the wrought-iron floral railings and general decorative style of the Casa Vicens (a sequence which even includes shots of a woman arranging flowers in a spacious front room). Ultimately, it is in its *mise en scène* that Teshigahara's film affirms a remarkable, improbable kinship between the Sōgetsu philosophy and the vision of Gaudí.

Liberated from the stultifying effects of voice-over narration, the images and sounds of *Antonio Gaudí* create meaning through allusion, juxtaposition, and association. The film is not an architectural guide to Gaudí, or a historical documentary outlining his contribution to the character of modern Barcelona: it is a documentary about the interaction of light, space, colour, and texture. Teshigahara trusts his audience to see the world for itself, to perceive the architectures of vision involved in regarding the real.

Notes

1 John Cage, 'How to Improve the World (You Will Only Make Matters Worse): Continued, 1967', *A Year from Monday: New Lectures and Writings* (Middletown, CT: Wesleyan University Press, 1967), p. 146.

2 William Klein, *Tokyo* (New York: Crown Publishers, 1964); David Campany, 'William Klein: Tokyo', *Photoworks*, 13 (2009), pp. 14–17.

3 While there is no major English-language study of SAC, the following relatively recent publications discuss its activities in relation to art and politics in post-war Tokyo: Richard R. H. Havens, *Radicals and Realists in the Japanese Non-Verbal Arts: The*

Avant-Garde Rejection of Modernism (Honolulu: University of Hawaii Press, 2006), pp. 102–15; Charles Merewether and Rika Lezumi Hiro, eds, *Art, Anti-Art, Non-Art: Experimentations in the Public Sphere in Postwar Japan: 1950-1970* (Los Angeles: Getty Research Institute, 2007); Doryun Chong, ed. *Tokyo: 1955–1970: A New Avant-Garde* (New York: MoMA, 2012); and William Marotti's *Money, Trains, and Guillotines: Art and Revolution in 1960s Japan* (Durham, NC: Duke University Press, 2013).

4   For a concise introduction to the aesthetics of *ikebana*, see Keiji Nishitani's 'The Japanese Art of Arranged Flowers', in *World Philosophy: A Text with Readings*, eds Robert C. Solomon and Kathleen M. Higgins (New York: McGraw-Hill, 1995), pp. 23–7.

5   Chong, *Tokyo: 1955–1970: A New Avant-Garde*, p. 70.

6   Qtd. in Dore Ashton's *The Delicate Thread: Teshigahara's Life in Art* (Tokyo: Kodansha, 1997), p. 63.

7   In 1949, the School of Fine Arts merged with the Music School to form the new Tokyo University of the Arts.

8   Henk Oosterling, 'Living – in between – Cultures: Downscaling Intercultural Aesthetics to Daily Life', in *Intercultural Aesthetics: A Worldview Perspective*, eds Antoon van den Braembussche, Heinz Kimmerle, Nicole Note (Springer: New York, 2009), p. 30.

9   The incident only became an international scandal after the publication of Ralph E. Lapp's *The Voyage of the Lucky Dragon* (New York: Harper, 1958). A distinguished US physicist, Lapp had worked on the Manhattan Project.

10 Salvador Dalí, 'Preface', in *Gaudí: The Visionary*, eds Robert Descharnes and Clovis Prévost, trans. Frederick Hill (London: Patrick Stephens, 1971), p. 6.

11 In 1963, Teshigahara made a short documentary on Jean Tinguely, the Swiss Neo-Dadaist kinetic artist and sculptor, who was exhibiting at Tokyo's Minami Gallery at that time, *Sculpture Mouvante: Jean Tinguely* (1981, JP, b&w, 15 min.). Tinguely – who constructed his sculptures from scrap metal – readily identified with SAC, and his work inspired several musical compositions by Ichiyanagi. Teshigahara's film collaborations with Kōbō Abe from this period are: *Pitfall/Otoshiana* (1962, JP, b&w, 97 min.); *The Woman in the Dunnes/Suna no onna* (1964, JP, b&w, 114 min.); *Face of Another/Tanin no Kao* (1966, JP, b&w, 124 min.); and *The Man without a Map/Moetsukita Chizu* (1968, JP, 118 min.). Takemitsu composed the scores for these films, and Segawa was the cinematographer for the first three (with Akira

Uehara replacing him for *The Man without a Map*, which was shot using Eastmancolor).

12   Hiroshi Teshigahara, 'My First Trip to the West', in *Antonio Gaudí* DVD booklet, trans. Juliet Winters Carpenter (Criterion, 2008), p. 16.

13   Gijs van Hensbergen, *Gaudí: A Biography* (London: Harper-Collins, 2001), p. 288, n. 44. See also Michel Tapié, *Gaudí: La Pedrera* (Barcelona: Ediciones Polígrafa, 1971); George R. Collins, *Antonio Gaudi* (New York: George Braziller, 1960); and James Johnson Sweeney and Josep Lluís Sert eds, *Antoni Gaudí* (New York: Praeger, 1960).

Bibliography

Aiken, Ian. *Film and Reform: John Grierson and the Documentary Film Movement*. London: Routledge, 1990.

Ali, Tariq. *Street Fighting Years: An Autobiography of the Sixties*. 2nd edn. London: Verso, 2005.

Allen, Steven and Hubner, Laura (eds). *Framing Film: Cinema and the Visual Arts*. Bristol: Intellect, 2012.

Andrew, Dudley (ed.). *The Image in Dispute: Art and Cinema in the Age of Photography*. Austin, TX: University of Texas Press, 1997.

Anthony, Scott and Mansell, James G. (eds). *The Projection of Britain: A History of the GPO Film Unit*. London: BFI/Palgrave, 2011.

Ashton, Dore (ed.). *A Joseph Cornell Album*. New York: Da Capo, 1974.

Ashton, Dore. *The New York School: A Cultural Reckoning*. Berkeley: University of California Press, 1992.

Ashton, Dore. *The Delicate Thread: Teshigahara's Life in Art*. Tokyo: Kodansha, 1997.

Aumont, Jacques. 'Point of View'. *Quarterly Review of Film and Video*, 11.2 (1989): 1–22.

Aumont, Jacques. *L'Œil interminable: cinéma et peinture*. Paris: Séguier, 1989.

Auster, Paul. *Collected Prose: Autobiographical Writings, True Stories, Critical Essays, Prefaces, Collaborations with Artists, and Interviews*. 2nd edn. New York: Picador, 2010.

Barthes, Roland. 'Lecture in Inauguration of the Chair of Literary Semiology, Collège de France, January 7, 1977'. Trans. Richard Howard. *October*, 8 (1979): 3–16.

Barthes, Roland. *Camera Lucida: Reflections on Photography*. Trans. Richard Howard. London: Jonathan Cape, 1982.

Barthes, Roland. *The Language of Fashion*. Eds Andy Stafford and Michael Carter. Trans. Andy Stafford. London: Berg, 2006.

Barthes, Roland. *What Is Sport?* Trans. Richard Howard. New Haven, CT: Yale University Press, 2007.

Beattie, Keith. *D. A. Pennebaker*. Champaign, IL: University of Illinois Press, 2011.

Belletto, Steven and Grausman, Daniel (eds). *American Literature and Culture in an Age of Cold War*. Iowa City: University of Iowa Press, 2012.

Bent, Jaap van der. '"O Fellow Travellers I Write You a Poem in Amsterdam": Allen Ginsberg, Simon Vinkenoog, and the Dutch Beat Connection'. *College Literature*, 27.1 (2000): 199–212.

Blair, Lindsay. *Joseph Cornell's Vision of Spiritual Order*. Edinburgh: Reaktion, 1998.

Bonfand, Alain. *Le Cinéma saturé: Essai sur les relations de la peinture et des images en mouvement*. Paris: PUF, 2007.

Bonitzer, Pascal. *Décadrages: Peinture et Cinéma*. Paris: Cahiers du cinéma/Éditions de l'Étoile, 1985.

Borges, Jorge Luis. *Jorge Luis Borges: Selected Non-Fiction*. Ed. Eliot Weinberger. New York: Penguin, 1999.

Bosworth, Richard (ed.). *The Oxford Handbook of Fascism*. Oxford: Oxford University Press, 2009.

Brenez, Nicole. '"The Ultimate Doomed Victims of the Romantic Dream": Jean-Luc Godard/Peter Whitehead', *Framework*, 52.1 (2011): 367–85.

Brenez, Nicole and Lebrat, Christian (eds). *Jeune, dure et pure! Une histoire du cinéma d'avant-garde et expérimental en France*. Paris/Milan: Cinématheque Française/Mazzotta, 2001.

Brenez, Nicole *et al.* (eds). *Jean-Luc Godard: Documents*. Paris: Centre Pompidou, 2006.

Brody, Richard. *Everything Is Cinema: The Working Life of Jean-Luc Godard*. New York: Henry Holt, 2008.

Brown, Simon. 'Dufaycolor: The Spectacle of Reality and British National Cinema'. AHRC Centre for British Television and Film Studies. 2005. www.bftv.ac.uk/projects/dufaycolor.htm#_ftn48

Burch, Noël. *Theory of Film Practice*. Trans. Helen R. Lane. New York: Praeger, 1973.

Burckhardt, Rudy and Pettet, Simon. *Talking Pictures: The Photography of Rudy Burckhardt*. Cambridge, MA: Zoland, 1994.

Burke, Patrick. 'Rock, Race, and Radicalism in the 1960s: The Rolling Stones, Black Power, and Godard's One Plus One'. *Journal of Musicological Research*, 29.4 (2010): 275–94.

Cage, John. *A Year from Monday: New Lectures and Writings*. Middletown, CT: Wesleyan University Press, 1967.

Cage, John. *John Cage*, ed. Richard Kostelanetz. New York: Praeger, 1970.

Campany, David. *Photography and Cinema*. Edinburgh: Reaktion, 2008.

Campany, David. 'William Klein: Tokyo'. *Photoworks*, 13 (2009): 14–17.

Caygill, Howard. 'Philosophy and the Black Panthers'. *Radical Philosophy*, 179 (2013): 7–13.

Chanan, Michael. 'Shooting Star: Peter Whitehead and the 1960s Documentary'. *Framework*, 52.1 (2011): 326–31.

Chong, Doryun (ed.). *Tokyo: 1955–1970: A New Avant-Garde*. New York: MoMA, 2012.

Clouzot, Claire. *William Klein: Films*. Paris: Maison Européenne de la Photographie, 1998.

Collins, George R. *Antonio Gaudi*. New York: George Braziller, 1960.

Cooper, Sarah. *Selfless Cinema? Ethics and French Documentary*. Oxford: Legenda, 2006.

Daney, Serge. *Postcards from the Cinema*. Trans. Paul Douglas Grant. Oxford: Berg, 2007.

Danto, Arthur C. *Unnatural Wonders: Essays from the Gap between Art and Life*. New York: Columbia University Press, 2005.

Danto, Arthur C. *Andy Warhol*. New Haven, CT: Yale University Press, 2009.

Darke, Chris. 'Three Images of May: Cinema and the Uprising'. *Vertigo*, 3.9 (2008), www.closeupfilmcentre.com/vertigo_mag azine/volume-3-issue-9-spring-summer-2008/three-images-of-may-cinema-and-the-uprising

Delorme, Stéphane. 'Cinéma ikebana'. *Cahiers du cinéma*, 632 (2008): 58.

Depardon, Raymond. *Notes*. Paris: Éditions Arfuyen, 1979.

Depardon, Raymond (with Alain Bergala). *Correspondance New-Yorkaise*. Paris: Libération/Éditions de l'Étoile, 1981.

Depardon, Raymond. *Voyages*. Paris: Hazan, 1998.

Depardon, Raymond. *Our Farm*. Arles: Actes Sud, 2006.

Depardon, Raymond. *Manhattan Out*. Guttenberg: Steidl, 2009.

Depardon, Raymond. *Paris Journal*. Paris: Hazan, 2010.

Derrida, Jacques. *Of Grammatology*. Trans. Gayatri Spivak. New edn. Baltimore, MD: Johns Hopkins University Press, 1998.

Derrida, Jacques. *Points ... Interviews, 1974–1994*. Ed. Elisabeth Weber. Stanford, CA: Stanford University Press, 1995.

Descharnes, Robert, and Prévost, Clovis (eds). *Gaudí: The Visionary*. Trans. Frederick Hill. London: Patrick Stephens, 1971.

Dieckmann, Katherine. 'Raging Bill: William Klein's Films'. *Art in America*, 78.12 (1990): 71–6.

Dika, Vera. *The (Moving) Pictures Generation: The Cinematic Impulse in Downtown New York Art and Film*. Basingstoke: Palgrave Macmillan, 2012.

Dyer, Geoff. *The Ongoing Moment*. London: Little, Brown, 2005.

Dyer, Geoff. *Working the Room*. Edinburgh: Canongate, 2010.

Edwards, Jason and Taylor, Stephanie (eds). *Joseph Cornell: Opening the Box*. Berlin: Peter Lang, 2007.

Elliott, Anthony. *The Mourning of John Lennon*. Berkeley, CA: University California Press, 1999.

Elsaesser, Thomas. *European Cinema: Face to Face with Hollywood*. Amsterdam: Amsterdam University Press, 2003.

Farber, Manny. *Negative Space: Manny Farber on the Movies*. 2nd edn. New York: Da Capo, 1998.

Farber, Manny, *Faber on Film: The Complete Film Writing of Manny Farber*. Ed. Robert Polito. New York: Library of America, 2009.

Fiedman, Ken (ed.). *The Fluxus Reader*. Chichester: Academic Editions/John Wiley, 1998.

Fogo, Fred. *'I Read the News': The Social Drama of John Lennon's Death*. Lanham, MD: Rowan & Littlefield, 1994.

Foster, Hal. 'Creaturely Cobra'. *October*, 141 (2012): 4–21.

Freud, Sigmund. *Standard Edition of the Complete Psychological Works of Sigmund Freud*. Vol. 19. Eds and trans. James Strachey and Anna Freud. London: Hogarth Press, 1971.

Godard, Jean-Luc, 'What Is to Be Done?' *Afterimage*, 1. (1970): npg.

Godard, Jean-Luc, *Godard on Godard: Critical Writings*. Eds Jean Narboni and Tom Milne. New York: Da Capo Press, 1986.

Godard, Jean-Luc, *Jean-Luc Godard: Interviews*. Ed. David Sterritt. Jackson, MS: University of Mississippi Press, 1998.

Godard, Jean-Luc, *The Future(s) of Film: Three Interviews: 2000–01*. Trans. John O'Toole. Bern: Verlag Gachnang & Springer, 2002.

Goldberg, Marcy. 'In the Arena: Interview with Ramón Gieling'. *Dox: Documentary Film Magazine*, 18 (1998): 18–19.

Grierson, John. *Grierson on Documentary*. Ed. Forsyth Hardy. London: Faber, 1979.

Hadouchi, Olivier. "'African Culture Will Be Revolutionary or Will Not Be": William Klein's Film of the First Pan-African Festival of Algiers (1969)'. *Third Text*, 25.1 (2011): 117–28.

Hagener, Malte. *Moving Forward, Looking Back: The European Avant-Garde and the Invention of Film Culture: 1919–1939*. Amsterdam: University of Amsterdam Press, 2014.

Harvey, Sylvia. *May '68 and Film Culture*. London: British Film Institute, 1978.

Hauptman, Jodi. *Joseph Cornell: Stargazing in the Cinema*. New Haven, CT: Yale University Press, 1999.

Hausheer, Cecilia and Settele, Christoph (eds). *Found Footage Films*. Zurich: Viper, 1992.

Havens, Thomas R. H. *Radicals and Realists in the Japanese Non-Verbal Arts: The Avant-Garde Rejection of Modernism*. Honolulu: University of Hawaii Press, 2006.

Henderson, Andrea and Katz, Vincent. *Picturing New York: The Art of Yvonne Jacquette and Rudy Burckhardt*. New York: Bunker Hill, 2008.

Hendricks, Geoffrey (ed.). *Critical Mass: Happenings, Performance, Fluxus, Intermedia, and Rutgers University: 1958–1972*. New Brunswick, NJ: Rutgers University Press, 2003.

Herskowitz, Richard (ed.). *Border Crossing: The Cinema of Johan van der Keuken*. Ithaca, NY: Herbert F. Johnston Museum of Art/ Cornell University, 1990.

Higgins, Hannah. *Fluxus Experience*. Berkeley, CA: University of California Press, 2002.

Hondius, Dienke. *Return: Holocaust Survivors and Dutch Anti-Semitism*. Westport, CT: Praeger, 2003.

Horrocks, Roger and Bonhours, Jean-Michel (eds). *Len Lye*. Paris: Centre Georges Pompidou, 2000.

Horrocks, Roger. *Len Lye: A Biography*. Auckland: University of Auckland Press, 2002.

Horrocks, Roger. *Art that Moves: The Work of Len Lye*. Auckland: Auckland University Press, 2013.

Hostetler, Lisa (ed.). *Street Seen: The Psychological Gesture in American Photography, 1940–1959*. New York: Prestel/Milwaukee Art Museum, 2010.

Jackson, Julian, Milne, Anna-Louise, and Williams, James S. (eds). *May '68: Rethinking France's Last Revolution*. Basingstoke: Palgrave Macmillan, 2011.

Jacobs, Steven. *Framing Pictures: Film and the Visual Arts*. Edinburgh: Edinburgh University Press, 2011.

James, David E. (ed.). *To Free the Cinema: Jonas Mekas and the New York Underground*. Princeton, NJ: Princeton University Press, 1992.

Klein, William. *Life Is Good and Good for You in New York: Trance Witness Revels*. Paris: Éditions du Seuil/Photography Magazine, 1956.

Klein, William. *Tokyo*. New York: Crown, 1964.

Klein, William. *William Klein: ABC*. London: Tate/Abrams, 2012.

Klimke, Martin, Pekelder, Jacco, and Scharloth, Joachim (eds). *Between Prague Spring and French May: Opposition and Revolt in Europe, 1960–1980*. Oxford: Berghan, 2011.

Kolker, Robert Philip and Cottenet-Hage, Madeleine. 'Godard's *Le Gai savoir*: A Filmic Rousseau?'. *Eighteenth Century Life*, 11 (1987): 117–22.

Kozloff, Max. *The Privileged Eye: Essays on Photography*. Albuquerque, NM: University of New Mexico Press, 1987.

Lapp, Ralph E. *The Voyage of the Lucky Dragon*. New York: Harper, 1958.

Lev, Peter. *Transforming the Screen: 1950–1959*. Berkeley, CA: University of California Press, 2003.

Linder, Christoph and Hussey, Andrew. *Paris–Amsterdam Underground: Essays in Cultural Resistance, Subversion, and Diversion*. Amsterdam: Amsterdam University Press, 2013.

Lippy, Tod (ed.). *Projections 11: New York Filmmakers on New York Filmmaking*. London: Faber, 2000.

Livingston, Jane. *The New York School: Photographs, 1936–63*. New York: Stewart, Tabori & Chang, 1992.

Low, Rachel. *The History of British Film*. 3 vols. London: Routledge, 1997 [1950].

Lucebert. *The Tired Lovers They Are Machines*. Trans. Peter Nijmeijer. London: Transgravity Press, 1974.

Lucebert. *Collected Poems: Volume 1: 1949–1952*. Trans. Diane Butterman. New York: Green Integer, 2010.

Lye, Len. *Figures of Motion: Selected Writings*. Eds Wystan Curnow and Roger Horrocks. Auckland: Auckland University Press, 1984.

MacCabe, Colin. *Godard: A Portrait of the Artist at Seventy*. London: Bloomsbury, 2003.

MacDonald, Scott (ed.). *A Critical Cinema: 2: Interviews with*

Independent Filmmakers. Vol. 2. Berkeley, CA: University of California Press, 1992.

MacDonald, Scott (ed.). *Avant-Garde Film: Motion Studies*. Cambridge: Cambridge University Press, 1993.

MacDonald, Scott (ed.). *A Critical Cinema: 3: Interviews with Independent Film-Makers*. Vol. 3. Berkeley, CA: University of California Press, 1998.

MacDonald, Scott. *The Garden in the Machine: A Field Guide to Independent Films about Place*. Berkeley, CA: University of California Press, 2001.

MacKenzie, Scott. 'The Missing Mythology: Barthes in Québec'. *Canadian Journal of Film Studies*, 6.2 (1998): 65–74.

McShine, Kynaston (ed.). *Joseph Cornell*. New York: MoMA, 1980.

Malina, Judith and Beck, Julian. *Paradise Now: Collective Creation of Living Theatre*. New York: Vintage, 1972.

Marotti, William. *Money, Trains, and Guillotines: Art and Revolution in 1960s Japan*. Durham, NC: Duke University Press, 2013.

Martin, Adrian. 'William Klein: Waiting for a Photographer'. Australian Centre for the Moving Image (ACMI), 2008, www.acmi.net.au/william_klein_essay.htm

Martinell, César. *Gaudí: His Life, His Theories, His Work*. Trans. Judith Rohrer. Ed. George R. Collins. Cambridge, MA: MIT Press, 1975.

Merewether, Charles and Hiro, Rika Lezumi (eds). *Art, Anti-Art, Non-Art: Experimentations in the Public Sphere in Postwar Japan: 1950–1970*. Los Angeles: Getty Research Institute, 2007.

Michelson, Annette. '*Rose Hobart* and *Monsieur Phot*: Early Films from Utopia Parkway'. *Artforum*, 11.10 (June 1973): 47–57.

Mollenkopf, John Hull (ed.). *Power, Culture, and Place: Essays on New York City*. New York: Russell Sage Foundation, 1988.

Mollenkopf, John Hull. *New York City in the 1980s: A Social, Economic, and Political Atlas*. New York: Simon & Schuster, 1993.

Muldoon, Paul. *The End of the Poem: Oxford Lectures*. London: Faber, 2006.

Murphet, Julian and Rainford, Lydia (eds). *Literature and Visual Technologies: Writing After Cinema*. Basingstoke: Palgrave Macmillan, 2003.

Nichols, Bill. *Representing Reality: Issues and Concepts in Documentary*. Bloomington, IN: Indiana University Press, 1991.

Nichols, Bill. 'Documentary Film and the Modernist Avant-Garde'. *Critical Inquiry*, 27.4 (2001): 580–610.

Norman, Philip. *John Lennon: The Life*. London: Harper, 2008.

O'Pray, Michael. *Avant-Garde Film: Forms, Themes, Passions*. London: Wallflower, 2003.

Perl, Jed. *New Art City: Manhattan at Mid-Century*. New York: Vintage, 2007.

Peucker, Brigitte. *The Material Image: Art and the Real in Film*. Stanford, CA: Stanford University Press, 2006.

Pigott, Michael. *Cornell versus Cinema*. London: Bloomsbury, 2013.

Rancière, Jacques. *Film Fables*. Trans. Emiliano Battista. Oxford: Berg, 2006.

Reader, Keith. *The May 1968 Events in France: Reproductions and Interpretations*. London: Macmillan, 1993.

Remy, Michel. *Surrealism in Britain*. Aldershot: Ashgate, 1999.

Renov, Michael. *The Subject of Documentary*. Minneapolis, MN: University of Minnesota Press, 2004.

Rohdie, Sam. *Intersections: Writings on Cinema*. Manchester: Manchester University Press, 2012.

Rosenbaum, Jonathan. *William Klein: Cinema Outsider*. Ex. Cat. Minneapolis, MN: Walker Art Center, 1989.

Rosenbaum, Jonathan. *Goodbye Cinema, Hello Cinephilia: Film Culture in Transition*. Chicago, IL: University of Chicago Press, 2010.

Roud, Richard. *Jean-Luc Godard*. London: BFI/Thames & Hudson, 1970.

Russell, Catherine. *Experimental Ethnography: The Work of Film in the Age of Video*. Durham, NC: Duke University Press, 1999.

Ryan, Michael. 'Militant Documentary: mai '68 par lui-même'. *Cine-Tracts*, 2.3–4 (1979): 1–20.

Scala, Mim. *Diary of a Teddy Boy: A Memoir of the Long Sixties*. London: Creative Space Independent Publishing, 2013.

Sexton, Jamie. *Alternative Film Culture in Inter-War Britain*. Exeter: Exeter University Press, 2008.

Siegelbaum, Sami. 'The Riddle of May '68: Collectivity and Protest in the Salon de la Jeune Peinture'. *Oxford Art Journal*, 35.1 (2012): 53–73.

Simic, Charles. *Dime-Store Alchemy: The Art of Joseph Cornell*. New York: NYRB, 1992.

Sitney, Adams P. *Modernist Montage: The Obscurity of Vision in Cinema and Literature*. New York: Columbia University Press, 1990.

Sitney, Adams P. *Visionary Film: The American Avant-Garde: 1943–2000*. 3rd edn. New York: Oxford University Press, 2002.

Sitney, Adams P. *Eyes Upside Down: Visionary Filmmakers and the Heritage of Emerson*. Oxford: Oxford University Press, 2009.

Smith, Alison. *French Cinema in the 1970s: The Echoes of May*. Manchester: Manchester University Press, 2005.

Smythe, Luke. 'Music and Image in Len Lye's Direct Films'. *Journal of New Zealand Art History*, 27 (2006): 1–14.

Smythe, Luke. 'Len Lye: The Vital Body of Cinema'. *October*, 144 (2013): 73–91.

Soloman, Deborah. *Utopia Parkway: The Life and Work of Joseph Cornell*. Boston, MA: Boston MFA, 1997.

Solomon, Robert C. and Higgins, Kathleen M. (eds). *World Philosophy: A Text with Readings*. New York: McGraw-Hill, 1995.

Sontag, Susan. *Essays of the 1960s & 1970s: Against Interpretation, Styles of Radical Will, on Photography, Illness as Metaphor, and Uncollected Essays*. Ed. David Rieff. New York: Library of America, 2013.

Stokvis, Willemijn. *Cobra: 1948–1951: A Return to the Sources of Art*. Zwolle, NL: Waanders, 2013.

Stone, Rob and Julian Daniel Gutierrez-Albilla. *A Companion to Luis Buñuel*. Oxford: Wiley-Blackwell, 2013.

Suarez, Juan A. *Pop Modernism: Noise and the Reinvention of the Everyday*. Champaign: University of Illinois Press, 2007.

Sussex, Elizabeth. *The Rise and Fall of the British Documentary: The Story of the Film Movement Founded by John Grierson*. Berkeley, CA: University of California Press, 1975.

Sweeney, James Johnson and Sert, Josep Lluís (eds). *Antoni Gaudí*. New York: Praeger, 1960.

Szwed, John. *So What: The Life of Miles Davis*. New York: Simon & Schuster, 2002.

Tapié, Michel. *Gaudí: La Pedrera*. Barcelona: Ediciones Polígrafa, 1971.

Temple, Michael and Witt, Michael (eds). *The French Cinema Book*. London: BFI, 2004.

Teshigahara, Hiroshi. 'My First Trip to the West [1986]'. *Antonio Gaudí* [DVD booklet]. Trans. Juliet Winters Carpenter. *Criterion* (2008), 14–19.

Thill, Brian. 'Black Power and the New Left: The Dialectics of Liberation, 1967'. *Mediations: Journal of the Marxist Literary Group*, 23.2 (2008): 119–34.

Thompson, Elizabeth and Gutman, David (eds). *The Lennon Companion: Twenty-Five Years of Comment*. London: Macmillan, 1987.

Thoreau, Henry D. *Walden*. Ed. Jeffrey Cramer. Intro. Denis Donoghue. New Haven, CT: Yale University Press, 2004.

Troy, Gil and Cannato, Vincent J. (eds). *Living in the Eighties*. Oxford: Oxford University Press, 2009.

Urbain, Jean-Didier. *At the Beach*. Trans. Catherine Porter. Minneapolis, MN: University of Minnesota Press, 2003.

Vacche, Angela Dalle (ed.). *Film, Art, New Media: Museum without Walls?* Basingstoke: Palgrave Macmillan, 2012.

Van den Braembussche, Antoon, Kimmerle, Heinz, and Note, Nicole. *Intercultural Aesthetics: A Worldview Perspective*. New York: Springer, 2009.

Van der Keuken, Johan. *Johan van der Keuken: The Lucid Eye: The Photographic Work, 1953–2000*. Amsterdam: De Verbeelding, 2001.

Van der Keuken, Johan. *Quatorze Juillet*. Amsterdam: Van Zoetendaal Gallery, 2010.

Van Hensbergen, Gijs. *Gaudí: A Biography*. London: Harper-Collins, 2001.

Van Zoetendaal, Willem. *To Sang*. Amsterdam: Basalt, 1995.

Vogel, Amos. *Film as a Subversive Art*. 2nd edn. New York: C. T. Editions, 2005.

Waard, Marco de (ed.). *Imagining Global Amsterdam: History, Culture, and Geography in a World City*. Amsterdam: Amsterdam University Press, 2012.

Wahlberg, Malin. *Documentary Time: Film and Phenomenology*. Minneapolis, MN: University of Minnesota Press, 2008.

Waldman, Diane. *Joseph Cornell: Master of Dream*. New York: Harry N. Abrams, 2006.

White, E. B. *Here Is New York*. New York: Little Bookroom, 1999.

Wiazemsky, Anne. *Une année studieuse*. Paris: Gallimard, 2012.

Wiener, Jon. *Come Together: John Lennon in His Time*. New York: Random, 1984.

Wiener, Jon. 'Pop and Avant-Garde: The Case of John and Yoko'. *Popular Music and Society*, 22.1 (1998): 1–18.

Williams, James S. '"C'est le petit livre rouge/Qui fait que tout enfin bouge": The Case for Revolutionary Agency and Terrorism in Jean-Luc Godard's *La Chinoise*'. *Journal of European Studies*, 40.3 (2010): 206–18.

Wilson, Sarah (ed.). *Revisions 2: Photogenic Painting: Gérard Fromanger*. London: Black Dog, 1999.

Winston, Brian. *Claiming the Real: The Griersonian Documentary and Its Legitimations*. 2nd edn. London: BFI, 2008.

Wollen, Peter. *Readings and Writings: Semiotic Counter-Strategies*. London: Verso, 1982.

Wollen, Peter. *Raiding the Icebox: Reflections on Twentieth Century Culture*. London: Verso, 1993.

Wollen, Peter. *Paris Hollywood: Writings on Film*. London: Verso, 2002.

Wollen, Peter. *Paris/Manhattan: Writings on Art*. London: Verso, 2004.

Zedong, Mao. *On Practice and Contradiction*. London: Verso, 2007.

Index